TEACH YOURSELF BOOKS

CRICKET

This book explains how t̶ ̶ ̶ ̶ ̶ ̶ ̶ ̶ ̶ ̶ ̶ ̶ ̶ ̶ ̶ ̶ ̶ ̶pire
cricket. Detailed inst̶ ̶ ̶ ̶ ̶ ̶ ̶ ̶ ̶ ̶ ̶ ̶ ̶ ̶ ̶
batting, bowling an̶ ̶ ̶ ̶ ̶ ̶ ̶ ̶ ̶ ̶ ̶ ̶ ̶ ̶
contains the curr̶ ̶ ̶ ̶ ̶ ̶ ̶ ̶

... A heap of useful advice complete with diagrams and illustrations that are both informative and simple to understand.

Manchester Evening News

TEACH YOURSELF BOOKS

CRICKET

F. N. S. Creek

R.A.F. XI, Wiltshire,
and B.B.C. Commentator

ST. PAUL'S HOUSE WARWICK LANE LONDON EC4P 4AH

First printed 1950
Second edition 1973
Third impression 1974

ISBN 0 340 17008 5

Printed and bound in England
for The English Universities Press Ltd
by Hazell Watson and Viney Ltd, Aylesbury

Contents

Acknowledgments

The author and publishers acknowledge with thanks permission to reproduce the photographs appearing in this book, which were supplied by Patrick Eagar and Central Press Photos Ltd.

They are also grateful to the M.C.C. for their kind permission to reproduce the current edition of the Laws of Cricket at the back of this book.

Picture research and captions by W. J. Bailey and D. Elwell.

CHAPTER I

How to Start

It is probably true of most games that the best way of starting to learn is to watch experts playing. This is certainly true of cricket, and all the more so for anyone who has to learn the game by himself. Yet unlike most other games, it is not necessary to watch the absolute top-notch expert. It is not necessary, for instance, to go to a Test Match or a county match in order to learn. A good club game, or, in certain places, a league game, or even a good secondary school game will prove quite as instructive in the technicalities, while a village match, though crude in technique, may give the spirit of the game best of all.

Let us first pay a visit to the headquarters of cricket, Lord's, and see what we can learn there. Arriving at St. John's Wood tube station in London, we walk down Wellington Road and enter the ground by the Wellington Place gate. We are at once presented with our first opportunity of profitable watching—the Nursery; in other words, the practice nets. Here, if we are in luck, we may get a close-up view of good bowlers and batsmen practising, or at least we may watch good bowlers bowling to learners of all ages and, perhaps, hear a good professional coaching.

After an instructive half-hour or so at the nets, we are summoned by an announcement over the loudspeaker telling us that Middlesex has won the toss and has elected to bat, so we hustle round to our seats in the stand resolving to pay as many more visits to the Nursery as circumstances allow. By the time we are seated and have bought a 'card of the match', it is almost 11.30 a.m., the umpires are coming out, and a policeman is quietly shooing the last small boy away to the boundary line round the edge of the playing field. Immediately after the umpires, the fielding side is led out of the enormous pavilion by their captain, quickly to be followed by the two opening batsmen. Number one 'takes guard' and carefully looks round the ground as the fieldsmen crouch or stride into their positions round him, and we settle ourselves into our seats for the first spell of play until lunch is taken.

The match card is devoid of scores as yet, but it gives us the names of the two batsmen who are carefully feeling their way against Surrey's opening bowlers. For the time being they are content to steal an occasional quiet single, and they are determined not to take any risks till they have mastered that sudden and uncomfortable lift off the pitch which the dew-affected wicket gives to some of the fast bowlers' deliveries. If we are a trifle uncertain as to which batsman is which, we need not be in doubt for long, as their numbers (1 and 2) are up on the great scoreboard crowned by the Father Time weather-vane, and it is only necessary for us to see whose total changes when a run is scored. The fielders are also given numbers on the card, lit electrically as required on the great scoreboard, so that it will eventually be possible to identify for ourselves all the players on both sides, even though we may have never seen them before.

Play is quiet on the whole. An occasional full toss or long hop is hit firmly to the boundary; one batsman snicks a ball which comes through quicker than he expected and a confident appeal of 'How's that' is answered by the umpire raising his finger and giving him out, caught at the wicket; another batsman mis-judges the slow bowler who has come on after forty minutes' play and he is well caught half way to the boundary. With the score at 100 for two wickets the players stroll off the field for the luncheon interval, and we are glad to pull out our sandwiches and to stretch our legs in a walk out to inspect the wicket. There we can see by tell-tale marks in the turf exactly where the fast bowler has been pitching his 'good length' ball, and are able to gauge by just how much the slow bowler varies his nearness to the stumps for different deliveries.

But soon the loud-speaker sends us back to our seats again for the long period of play until tea is taken. This is the most gruelling time for the players, and when it is very hot there is often a pause while drinks are brought out to them. The tea interval is soon over and play goes on until the shadows lengthen and the sun sinks behind the stands, while the seats begin to empty as their occupiers leave for early buses or trains; and at last the players stroll from the field at the close of the day's play.

There are two more days of the match to watch if we have the leisure to do so and during these we shall be able to bask in the gentle atmosphere of cricket and soak ourselves in the deep waters of its technique. You may be certain that there will be thrills and excitement; it is very seldom that a cricket match cannot provide these for the informed watcher of the game. To him, as also to every man on the field, each ball that is bowled has the makings of some thrill, though we must not be continually expecting such obvious ones as the fall of a wicket or the hitting of a six. In any case, both of these are often the cumulative result of careful preparation in preceding balls.

And what may we have gained from our day's watching? The answer depends largely on the standard of our cricketing experience or on our own practical ability in the various departments of the game. Perhaps we have been lucky and have seen two famous players in a big partnership, lucky but a little bewildered by the wealth of scoring strokes which we have seen. Or we may, again with luck, have had a seat nearly behind the bowlers and have seen how one of them brings his arm over for an 'in-swinger', or where another pitches the ball for his leg-breaks. Or we may have left our seat and wandered round the ground, getting glimpses from different positions which gave us clearer impressions of the bowler's length, or how far back the wicket-keeper stands for the fast bowler, or the relative positions of various fielders. Or we may have gained nothing more than a near view of a good deep fielder taking a high catch, so that we could watch how he moved and held his hands. Whatever it is, if we wish to learn from our watching, we must try to go home with a clear picture of what we have seen and with a determination to try it out ourselves at the earliest opportunity.

The same technical skills can also be learnt by watching club cricket or good school cricket, where the spirit is often lighter-hearted but where stylish play is often more evident and—this is of greater importance perhaps —where it is possible to get a nearer view of the batsmen and bowlers than one can from the stands of a large county ground. In this type of cricket, where two innings can be completed in one day or even in an afternoon, the scoring is usually faster and the players more generally active than in first-class cricket, where players have to conserve their energy so as to be able to last out the long and arduous season without tiring. Many people find this more entertaining to watch than the slower progress of first-class cricket, but as methods of learning they are different only in the things that can best be learnt from them. For those who have sufficient knowledge of the rules of the game, the most profitable instruction is obtained by watching the umpire.

League cricket, especially in Yorkshire and Lancashire, is also worth watching, both for its technical skill and for the keenness with which every point of the game is contested and every rule closely adhered to. It numbers amongst its players some of the highest paid professionals in the game, and it attracts, therefore, many great players with international reputations from Australia, South Africa and the West Indies, as well as from England.

Cricket at its most boisterous but least skilful can best be seen at a village cricket match in the country. Here the pitch is often so deceptive and the outfield so tangled and long that to attempt a defensive stroke is a waste of time and any scoring shot that is not lofted so as to pass over the arresting long grass is a waste of energy. Nevertheless, it is probably here that one can see the true and original spirit of cricket, with its physical boldness and keen competition, and without all the modern trappings that have tended to make it a spectacle rather than a game. The scores are low, for no one stays in long when the ball does such uncalculated breaks and shoots off the pitch at such varying paces. The fielders' movements are tense but ungainly, for who can move gracefully over uneven ground covered by long grass? The bowlers, fast or slow, with hardly an exception use a very short run, dictated by the nearness of the edge of the long grass to the bowling crease. The umpires often show so little knowledge of the rules that it is generally fatal for a batsman to allow any ball to hit him on the body! The spectators consist of a highly critical row of old gentlemen who really do know something about this sort of cricket, having played on this same ground thirty, forty or even fifty years ago when the conditions were even more difficult and dangerous!

In conclusion—a word of advice to the watcher-learner. Unless you are watching for the purpose of learning something about the general principles of the game, you should steel yourself to look for only one thing at a time. If it is bowling, keep your eye on the bowler only, and the same if wicket-keeping, or batting, or fielding is your prime interest of the moment. You will find that your eye will tend to want to follow the ball, but that instinct must be resisted until it is possible for you to say of a bowler 'Yes, that's his in-swinger' or 'That's his leg-break'; of a batsman 'Ah! That was a drive between cover and extra cover'; or of a fieldsman 'He missed that because he held his hands wrongly' or 'What a bad throw-in—his position was all wrong'; and all that, perhaps, without ever seeing the ball through your field-glasses. In fact, the best general rule for the watcher-learner is to take a pair of binoculars and 'watch the man and not the ball'.

CHAPTER 2

A Brief History of Cricket

Modern cricket has developed from a crude game which was played as early as the 12th century; but the first real cricket club to be established was the Hambledon Club, which flourished in the second half of the 18th century. This was followed, in 1787, by the Marylebone Cricket Club, which later made its headquarters at Lord's in St. John's Wood, London; and since that day the M.C.C. has been the recognized authority on all cricket affairs.

The game was originally played on ordinary English meadow-land, with long uncut grass for the outfield, and only the actual pitch was scythed. Later, light wooden rollers were used on the wicket, sheep were used to keep the grass down to a reasonable height and a 'boundary line' was marked all round the field. These improvements made for much higher scoring, because not only did the ball run over the ground much easier but also the batsmen did not become so tired when it became no longer necessary to run out the 'boundaries'. The next step was the inclusion of a rule which allowed the actual pitch to be brushed, swept and rolled after each innings. Later still, the hand mower made another big improvement, first to the state of the wicket and then to the whole outfield. The scoring was originally done by a 'notcher', who cut a notch in a stick whenever a run was scored. Village cricket in Kent and Sussex was probably the first true home of the game, which steadily grew and developed, in spite of a rather dark period when a considerable amount of gambling and wagering on results took place.

A great deal of the history of cricket can be learned from a visit to the pavilion of the present Lord's Cricket Ground. Thomas Lord was the original owner of the ground; he took it over in 1814 after he had owned previous cricket grounds in Dorset Square and North Bank, and it has been known as Lord's ever since. Let us go in imagination into the pavilion and have a look at some of the interesting things inside. As we go up the steps from the playing field through rows and rows of seats, we come into what is known as the 'Long Room'. This has gigantic windows, behind which are long rows of chairs for members who prefer to watch the cricket from indoors; the front row chairs are of ordinary height, while the back row consists of special high ones so that the members can see in comfort over the heads of those in front. Notices say 'Please do not move behind the bowler's arm', and you have to be careful not to wander about in the Long Room, as there are no sight-screens at the pavilion end.

The Long Room contains many portraits of great cricketing personalities, including Thomas Lord himself, W. G. Grace, Mann, Parr and Wisden, as well as many relics in glass cases. In one case is a cricket ball with a stuffed sparrow perched on it and the caption reads 'This sparrow was killed at Lord's by a ball bowled by Jahangir Khan of Cambridge University to T. N. Pearce, M.C.C., on July 3rd, 1936'—jolly bad luck to have been killed by that million to one chance! Another interesting object is a peculiar wooden instrument, a cross between a cricket bat and a boomerang. Apparently a team of Australian aborigines came over to this country in 1868, and one of them, rejoicing in the name of 'Dick-a-dick', was so clever with this bat-like weapon that he could defend himself with it while dozens of cricket balls were thrown at him!

In the next case is a beautiful cup made from an emu's egg; it has silver edges and was presented to the manager of the first English team to visit Australia in 1862. Nearby is a little urn containing the famous 'Ashes'. These ashes are, of course, only a symbol, because after Murdoch's team from Australia beat England in 1882, English cricket was said to have died and the body cremated, so that the ashes could be taken back to Australia. Later when the Hon. Ivo Bligh's team won a series of matches out there, some Australian ladies burnt a cricket stump, and the ashes were placed in the tiny but now precious little urn, only about 4 inches high, and they were triumphantly brought back to England. As a result of this, whenever England and Australia play each other at cricket, we always refer to 'The Fight for the Ashes'.

Further along, we can see a case of cricket caps. Some are old ones, like the ones which telegraph boys wear nowadays, and some are modern ones like the present-day England caps, the 'touring' ones with the crest of St. George and the Dragon, and the 'home' ones emblazoned with three lions. Next we notice a lot of interesting old balls and bats; an 1820 ball, very similar to the ones we use today, only lighter in colour, and heavy curved bats which gradually got straighter as the years went on. The reason for this was that originally there were only two stumps at each end of the pitch, with one long bail across the top. All bowling was underhand and often close to the ground, and as there was often a doubt as to whether the ball had gone *through* the wicket between the two stumps, a centre stump was added. At the same time, as fewer 'daisy cutters' were bowled along the ground, the curvature on the bats became less and less until the modern straight ones resulted.

Next we see the bat with which Albert Trott actually hit a ball, when playing against Australia in 1890, clean over the Lord's pavilion, an enormous drive which has never been repeated. Next to it, by way of contrast, is a flimsy looking bat carved out of an old packing-case and used by British soldiers when they were prisoners-of-war in Italy in 1942; it is autographed all down the front, just as some famous Test Match bat might be.

Amongst the many interesting paintings in the Long Room is one of Lord's in 1837, showing the M.C.C. Jubilee match—North versus South—in progress. If we look at it very carefully, we can see a pleasant little pavilion, rather like a modern school cricket pavilion, a big flagstaff with an enormous flag flying, spectators sitting on benches—one onlooker at deep mid-on is actually seated on a horse!—the bowler, just about to deliver the ball underhand, has carefully placed his top-hat on the ground some distance behind the wicket, and the fielders all seem very much on the alert. It also strikes us how very similar the fieldsmen's positions were compared with what they would be today; the painting shows seven fielders on the off side and only two on the leg, and although the wicket-keeper is standing quite close up to the wicket, neither he nor the batsmen are wearing any pads.

Another painting of an old game in progress shows the fielders trying to run out a batsman by placing the ball in the block-hole before he can get his bat there. That reminds us of the days when there used to be a block-hole in between the two original stumps, instead of on the popping crease as we have today; the fieldsmen used to scramble to place the ball in that hole while the batsman was running and no doubt they often got their fingers rapped when short runs were being stolen. All these features are to be found in that great 'museum' of cricket—the pavilion at Lord's; and they certainly teach us a good deal about the history of the game. Outside, on the field itself, we find things very different from a description which Dr. Grace gave in the early sixties. He claimed that the ground was in a very unsatisfactory condition, partly due to the fact that the creases were not chalked out but were actually cut out of the turf 1 inch deep and about 1 inch wide. No pains, he said, were taken to fill up the holes and batsmen were constantly damaged by fast bowling.

In the early days, it must be remembered, all bowling was underhand, but in 1825 'round arm' bowling was permitted; this meant that the ball could be delivered at any angle so long as the hand was not above the elbow. The chief result of this was that bowling became faster but less accurate, and many balls were so erratic that they beat both the wicket-keeper and his assistant, the 'long-stop'. After 1865, when 'over-hand' bowling was legalized, 'lobs' and 'round arm' bowling gradually died out. Most of the players, though, were still classed as either batsmen or bowlers, and it was not until the end of the 19th century that the 'all-rounder' began to appear, with a consequent stiffening of the middle of the batting order.

The actual origin of over-arm bowling is uncertain, although a certain John Willes of Sutton Valence is often given the credit for discovering it. It is said that he got the idea from his sister when she bowled—or probably threw—at him in practice. Orthodox bowling at the time was still underhand, and when, in one important match at Lord's, Willes was no-balled for his new action, the story goes that he flew into such a temper that he jumped on his horse, rode out of the ground and never played cricket again! Yet in spite of incidents like that, the bowling arm got gradually higher and higher until no umpire dared to no-ball the bowlers.

While the bats and other accessories have altered

greatly during the last hundred years, there has been little change in the actual balls. Except for the finish and the more polished appearance, a modern cricket ball is almost identical to the ones used at the beginning of the 19th century. In fact, in 1811, a Mr. Duke of Penshurst in Kent stated that his family had been making cricket balls for 250 years—crimson leather covers over hemp or hair stuffing—so that takes us back to about 1560. Before that, tennis balls were used for cricket when it was played indoors by both ladies and gentlemen; the poorer folk played it outside in the fields, where the tree 'stumps' would make a handy wicket. This applied particularly in the regions of the Kent and Sussex ports, where the shipbuilders of those days had cut down so many trees.

It is a far cry from those primitive days to our highly organized modern cricket matches. The laws and conditions of play are constantly changing as the years go by, but the spirit of the game remains unchangeable.

CHAPTER 3

Batting

Far more time is spent by cricket coaches on batting
than on any other part of the game. How, then, can
you hope to teach yourself? In general, by watching
good players, by practising in front of a mirror without
a ball, in nets (or their substitute) with a ball, and by a
certain amount of reading. The experience and practice
of games and matches is, of course, the finishing school,
but batting has the peculiar disadvantage that the better
the player the more practice in games he will get, and,
conversely, the poorer the player the less time he is
likely to have at the wicket! It is for this reason that the
actual game or match must be regarded as the finishing
school. It is going to be assumed throughout this chapter
that, unless the text indicates otherwise, the reader is a
naturally right-handed batsman. Most of the statements
referring to hands, wrists, arms and feet must therefore
be reversed if you bat left-handed.

It is well to realize from the very beginning that the
batting strokes are often unnatural movements for us.
If you are going to bat right-handed, it is—rather
paradoxically—the left hand which has to be in control.
When you consider that, during the one or two seconds
which the ball takes to travel from the bowler's hand to
the batsman, the latter has to estimate what is the
direction and length of the ball, to decide what stroke
to play, and to communicate to his arms and legs the
necessary movements to complete that stroke, you will
realize that batting is an excellent example of the rapid

co-ordination between mind and limb. Without making the art of batting seem any more complicated, let us start from the beginning by considering the batsman's equipment.

Batting gloves, pads and bat

Although the above articles of equipment are written down in order of increasing importance, all normal players use all three. Many boys disdain to use batting gloves, even when they are provided; perhaps when they start to play the game, the bowling is of such a moderate pace that a few knocks from the ball are no more painful than other knocks they are used to take in the ordinary run of life. But as they meet faster and faster bowling, the use of gloves becomes a sensible practice. To a smaller extent, the same attitude may apply to the use of pads, but since footwork is the all-important part of batting, there must be no excuse for wanting to get your legs out of the way of the ball. Apart from the fact that the pads should be the right size and comfortable, there is little more to mention, except that wicket-keeping pads (with extra width) should not be used for batting.

The choice of bat is most important. First, it must be just the correct size and weight. Many boys are handi-capped from the start by being given a bat that is too heavy for them. The idea is that they will grow into it by next year, but the trouble is that by next year their batting will probably have been spoilt. To play with a bat that is too light or small does not matter so much, except that when a player later adopts the proper size, he may want to hold it too far down the handle. The vital point is that the bat should have the right weight and length for the strength and height of the user. The following is given as an approximate guide:

Size of Bat	Weight	Length	Height of User	Age
Full Size	2·4 lb	2 ft 11 in	5 ft 9 in+	⎫ MAN
'Short Handle'	2·4 lb	2 ft 10 in	5 ft 7 in	⎬
Harrow	2·3 lb	2 ft 10 in	5 ft 5 in	16+
6	2·2 lb	2 ft 9 in	5 ft 2 in	15
5	1·8 lb	2 ft 7½ in	5 ft 0 in	13+

If you do not possess a bat of your own, the practice exercises which are described later can quite easily be carried out with an old discarded bat. Such a bat would no doubt have some crack which would prevent it from being used in a proper game, and it would probably be too large for you. Any carpenter could cut it off to the right length and plane it down to the right weight. As far as possible, the point of balance should be kept at the usual place, that is about 13 to 14 inches from the bottom. It will in no way matter if the bat is made narrower than the normal 4¼ inches. In this process of doctoring a discarded bat, its former crack may have been removed together with the wood that has gone into shavings. Anyhow, a handle to grasp and a blade to swing are the main necessities for learning how to bat.

If you are fortunate enough to possess a proper bat of your own, a few hints on looking after it will not be amiss:

1. A new bat must be carefully 'broken in'.

(a) Oil the front face about half-way up from the bottom.

(b) Hit the part of the bat where most balls are going to be played, either with a ball in your hand or with a special form of small mallet whose head is shaped like the surface of a ball.

(*c*) Use the bat for a series of gentle strokes in the nets.

(*d*) Oil again, and repeat (*b*) and (*c*).

This process should continue for a week or two before the bat should be used in a serious game, the time depending on the softness of the wood.

2. Oil a bat whenever it may become dry—preferably with linseed oil—but remember that too much oil will make a bat too heavy, like a log.

3. When the surface has become so hard that it does not soak in the oil, the hard outer surface must be removed by scraping with a glass edge or similar scraper.

4. To preserve the rubber handle as long as possible, keep the bat in the dark when out of use, certainly not in the hot sun.

Holding the bat

There are several vital preliminaries for batting which, if disregarded in the first stages, may be the causes of many future troubles; one of these is the correct way to hold the bat. It is unlikely that a verbal description will produce quite the desired result, so the best way is to show your grip to someone who knows how a bat *should* be held and ask for his opinion.

The grip is really quite a natural one. The left hand is, of course, above the right, and the hands should be together towards the top of the handle; if you really have to use a bat that is too long, you will have to correct that by holding it half-way down the handle. The back of the left hand should be facing towards the bowler or mid-off and not turned round in the direction of point. Both thumbs must be round the handle, not pointing down it. As a rough test for your grip being natural, lift the bat straight up in front of you so that it comes over your right shoulder, just as if it were a sledge hammer with which you intend to knock in a post in front of you. (The edge of your bat, not the face, would hit the post.) If your grip is the natural one for that sledge hammer work, then it is very near the proper one for batting, although a few minor adjustments will be necessary according to your stance and the position of your left arm. Hold firm with all the fingers of the *left* hand, but only with the thumb and first finger of the *right* hand; this is because the left hand has to control the movements of the bat. Be careful not to allow your hands to slip apart on the handle; in the early stages it is a good tip to keep on feeling for the first finger of your left hand with the little finger of your right hand.

The stance

Like the grip, the stance should be quite natural and easy. The main aim is to be able to move either foot freely, as required for each stroke; consequently, the weight should be distributed *evenly* beween the two feet. Stand up close to your bat, and do not bend your knees or crouch. The right foot should be just about parallel to the crease; this helps the shoulders to point almost straight down the pitch towards the bowler. Some players keep their two feet together; others prefer them some distance apart; that is immaterial.

You will probably have heard about avoiding a 'two-eyed stance'. This is an unfortunate phrase, because every player turns his head so that he uses both eyes to follow the flight of the ball. What is usually meant by a two-eyed stance is one in which the left shoulder, instead of pointing towards the bowler, points to mid-on, thus making the stance what is called 'open'. Such a stance will cramp you for driving balls to the off and is really only suitable for playing every ball to the leg.

Watching a batsman

It is now time to study a good batsman and his methods. To watch from the boundary of a county ground is rather too far away, at any rate without the aid of field-glasses. It has already been explained that binoculars are a great help because they make you concentrate on the movements of the player while ignoring the actual movement of the ball. In the early stages you will learn more by watching at close quarters not necessarily first-class players but any with a good style, such as the best bats of a school eleven or members of a good club side. There are two ways of watching at close quarters; one is to stand behind the nets when practice is taking place and the other is to umpire a game. By a keen study of the laws and advice on their interpretation, anyone after a little experience will be welcomed as an umpire for games; it is for that reason that a chapter is given later to umpiring.

By whatever method you find it possible to watch a good batsman, there are a number of distinct points to study, and it is best to concentrate on one of them at a time. The first step is to sort out a batsman's strokes and to see when he uses each one, according to the bowling served up to him. Always remember that a batsman's aim is two-fold: firstly, to score runs and, secondly, to avoid getting out. As will be mentioned later under 'General Tactics', the first of these aims is sometimes much more important and sometimes much less important than the second; it all depends on the state of the game at any particular moment. Under *normal* playing conditions, they are of approximately the same importance; therefore the batsman's mental attitude should be as follows:

'This ball is a good ball. I will just aim at preventing it taking my wicket.' Or—'This ball is not on the right line to bowl me, but there is very little chance of my scoring off it. I will therefore not attempt anything, but I will either play it quietly or else let it go past altogether.' Or—'This ball just suits one of my scoring strokes. I am justified in playing such a stroke.'

The fascination of cricket is that it consists of a number of justifiable risks and justifiable precautions being taken; and so, when you think of it, are many of our actions of everyday life. It is always a risk to cross a busy thoroughfare, but it is a justifiable risk if you look and act properly; it is an unjustifiable risk if you do not look but just dash across. You will find many unjustifiable risks taken in cricket; sometimes the player is lucky, sometimes unlucky, but, after all, it is only a game, so that the consequences are not fatal or serious. Now let us see what type of balls the batsman puts into the different categories and illustrate them by diagrams.

Good balls that must be treated with care

The bowler will normally aim at bowling the balls shown in the following diagrams. The good length ball, after bouncing, could only be met on the upper half of the bat, that is above the driving part, and therefore it is especially difficult to score off such a ball, even when it is not straight. Moreover, after the ball has pitched, there is a very small interval of time in which to watch the ball before it has to be played. The ball which pitches just about on the crease is called a 'Yorker'. Such a ball can only be played right at the bottom of the bat and cannot be driven, although a first-class batsman could possibly glide the ball on one side or other of the wicket.

If either a yorker or a good length ball is straight, that

is on the line of the wicket, you will find that the good batsman concentrates on stopping the ball from hitting his wicket. If a good length ball is on the off side, the batsman will probably be seen to let it go past without attempting a stroke, because he knows he cannot score off that type of ball and he could very easily give a catch if he did make a stroke. A yorker off the wicket will probably be treated as if it were a full pitch, and the batsman is safe in attempting to hit it.

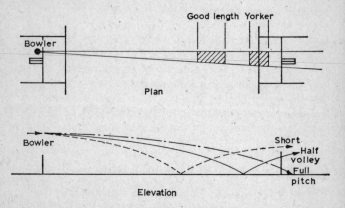

The next important fact to observe is that for playing the straight balls the bat is kept in a vertical plane while it is moved back and then forward to meet the ball. This vertical position of the bat is commonly called 'playing a straight bat', which, when you come to think about it, is rather a foolish phrase. You will clearly appreciate that the straight bat gives the best chance of the batsman covering his wicket and making contact with the ball, provided that the bat is swung like a pendulum along the line of flight of the ball. Here are two simple diagrams to show the relative values of a 'straight' and 'cross' bat:

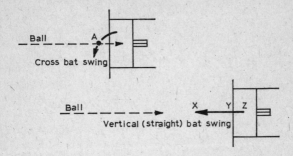

| A is the only place at which bat and ball can come into contact, so that a cross-bat swing demands perfect timing, with the chances against the ball being hit at all. | In the region of Z the ball will be hit *into* the ground, at Y it will be driven *along* the ground and at X it will be hit *into the air*. But the point is that the ball *will* be hit. |

Balls from which the batsman scores runs

Balls which do not pitch in the areas which are shaded in the diagram on page 28 fall into three classes:

1. Full pitches—any ball pitched beyond the length of a yorker.
2. Half-volleys—balls pitched beyond the good length but not as far as the yorker.
3. Short balls—any ball pitched short of a good length.

It should be realized that the exact position of the good length area depends both on the speed of the bowler and on the pace of the wicket; this will be explained more fully in the chapter on bowling. Here are the corresponding diagrams for these three classes of 'loose' balls:

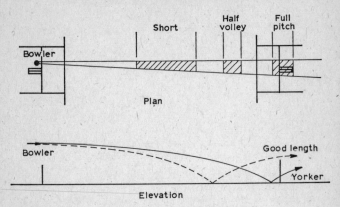

The trajectories represented above are those delivered by a medium-to-fast bowler, for it is in that case that short balls go over the top of the wicket after bouncing. Now observe how these balls are played. The vertical bat is still used for the balls on the wicket or roughly as far as a foot to either side of the middle stump, but when the balls are further than that from the wicket a cross-bat stroke is made, deliberately.

So far you have been asked to observe how the bat meets or strikes the ball, in other words how the hands and arms control the bat; but you will no doubt have also observed that the batsman moves his feet in a variety of ways. These movements can also be classified. For balls that are short, the batsman will first move his *right* foot back towards the wicket. For all balls that are half-volleys, yorkers or full pitches, he will move his *left* foot forward and the arms will follow forward. In this way, then, we find that a batsman uses four fundamental strokes:

1. Playing back at balls near the line of the wickets.
2. Playing forward at balls near the line of the wickets.

3. Cross-bat strokes at balls wide on the off side.
4. Cross-bat strokes at balls on the leg side.

To these must be added a fifth stroke:

5. Running out to drive or play slow bowling.

It is necessary to teach yourself these five strokes, remembering that in each case this means movement of both feet and arms. We will suppose that first of all you are on your own and have no one to bowl or throw balls for you to hit. The process will be divided for convenience and reference into a series of lessons.

1st Exercise. Learning to swing the bat for vertical strokes

This is an exercise for the left hand only, if you have sufficient strength; if not, the right can assist to a small extent. If possible, you should stand in front of a mirror so that you can see yourself playing while looking forward in the normal way as you watch the imaginary ball coming towards you. Take up your stance as recommended in the previous section. Pay special attention to the grip of the bat by your left hand. Now lift the bat back in a straight line (towards your stumps), bend your left elbow, allow the forearm to reach the horizontal and bend the left wrist slightly so that the bat almost reaches the vertical. The right hand can help this lift of the bat, but only by gripping with the thumb and first finger.

Now for the forward swing. Just let the bat swing down to its starting point, but then let its momentum carry the left arm forward *away* from the body. The left arm remains quite straight and the back of the hand faces forwards and then upwards. This forward motion of the arm can reach an almost horizontal position. From the forward position, the arm swings back to the starting point; in this way you can let the bat swing backwards and forwards, allowing it to hang down vertically at the bottom of the swing. The whole object of this swinging exercise without the right hand is that the weight of the bat is bound to carry it into the desired vertical position. Look into your mirror to make sure that is so. Remember that, when a bat is gripped by *both* hands, the two hands have sufficient strength to move it in any position, and the most natural motion is something like the mowing action of a scythe. This type of stroke is useless for cricket, and by this time you have probably proved to yourself that it is the right hand that causes all the trouble.

2nd Exercise. The first stage of the back stroke

Take up your normal stance again. Lift the bat back as in the first exercise, then swing it down, at the same time raising the left hand so that the bat will be able to play a ball 2 to 3 feet above the ground. When the left hand moves upwards, the left elbow has to bend and keep well away from the left side of the body. If the elbow points upwards, your left wrist will be able to keep in its normal line with the forearm, but if the elbow points forwards, the left wrist will have to bend in order to keep the bat in its vertical position. For short balls that rise high, the elbow usually points upwards, while for the short ball that keeps lower, the elbow points forwards. The bat should continue to be swung backwards and forwards in the way described until the movement becomes a comfortable and free one. If you stand in front of a mirror, you can see whether the bat is moving in the vertical plane. Be sure that the left elbow gets away from your left side; it is a common fault for it to be tucked in to the body. Here is a simple test for this: start with a small cushion held between the body and the upper part of the left arm; if you carry out a back stroke with the cushion still held, then the left arm is *not* moving correctly.

3rd Exercise. The complete back stroke

Having practised the arm movement by itself, you must now try to combine it with the footwork. Just before the bat is moved, the right foot moves to its right about 10 to 14 inches and slightly forwards, that is in front of the line of the wickets. As the bat moves down, all the weight is transferred back on to the right foot, so that

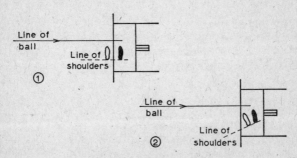

MOVEMENT OF THE FEET IN BACK STROKE

the left foot just hangs in the air or is just touching the ground. The right leg is straight—not bent at the knee—and the weight is on the ball of the foot. There are two reasons for this: firstly, your eye—and therefore your head—must be moved right on to the line of the on-coming ball; secondly, you may want to move slightly further to the off side, and this can be achieved by a sway when you are poised on the ball of your right foot.

The upper part of your body hardly moves *back* at all,
but the shoulders will turn round so that their line is
more across than down the wicket.

4th Exercise. Practising the back stroke

If you are still on your own and without a friend to
bowl suitable balls to you, you can take a string bag,
place a cricket ball in it, and hang the bag up by the
long string to any suitable support, so that the ball is
about two feet from the ground. Then stand beside the
ball and use the back stroke to hit it gently. As the ball
swings forward, transfer the weight on to both feet, and
then, as the ball comes towards you again, move the
right foot so as to bring your head along the line of flight
of the ball and play another stroke. You will find that
the swinging ball will come in various directions towards
you, giving you practice at back play on both the leg and
off sides of your imaginary wicket. When the motion of
the ball is no longer towards you, it must be stopped and
a fresh start made.

Playing forward

When a player judges that the oncoming ball is going
to pitch beyond the good length, he prepares to play
forward. For a moment all the weight is put on to the
right foot, so that the left foot is free to move forward.
The bat is taken back as for the back stroke, except that
a rather shorter back lift is recommended when playing
fast bowling, and then it is swung down in the same way
as in the exercise for swinging the bat. The left hand
controls the motion of the bat, the right hand only gripping with the thumb and first finger until the bat is near
the vertical position when it is about to hit the ball.
Just as the bat is starting to move down, the left foot
moves forward in such a way that the ball will just miss

hitting your pad, allowing the bat to swing alongside the foot and strike the ball. The left foot is bent at the knee and all weight is transferred to it, so that the right foot is just touching the ground at the toe. When you practise this lunge, make sure that a portion of the right foot really does touch the ground inside the batting crease, otherwise a good wicket-keeper will have you stumped whenever you miss the ball. The body should be bent forward so that the head comes right over the bat as it plays the ball; this is most important. Remember, too, that if the ball is played in front of the left leg, instead of alongside it, you are very liable to give an easy catch back to the bowler.

5th Exercise. Practising the forward stroke

As the most important part of the forward stroke is co-ordinated movement of foot and arms, the following simple exercise is suggested. It consists merely of hitting balls which are stationary on the ground. Four balls are required, but they need not necessarily be cricket balls; cheap rubber ones will do.

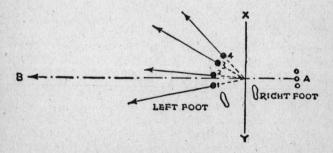

It is worth while to mark out in some way the line XY, representing the crease, and the line AB from the middle stump at A towards the middle stump of the other wicket. Place the four balls in the positions 1, 2, 3 and 4, so that 1 represents a ball on the leg side, 2 a straight ball, and 3 and 4 balls on the off side. The distance of the balls from the crease is the same as your left foot can comfortably lunge forward. Take up your normal stance, lift the bat back towards the stumps, have a look at the bat in that position to see that it is correct, move your left foot just beside ball 1 and at the same time swing the bat down to hit that ball to mid-on. See that your head is over the ball when it is hit. Return to your starting position and deal with balls 2, 3 and 4 in a similar way. You will find that a nice adjustment of arms and wrist is necessary in order to hit the ball cleanly without digging into the ground. As this adjusting of wrists has to be made when actually playing a moving ball, the exercise is a suitable one. When the left foot is moved, do not point the toe towards the bowler but let it point in the same direction as for your stance. The reason for this is that, if the left foot is pointed, it makes your left shoulder swing round, and that, in turn, causes the bat to swing across the proper line.

Now when you have been watching some batting, or even listening to a running commentary on the game, you will realize that there are two types of forward stroke. 'He just played that ball by a forward defensive stroke and the ball has gone gently down to mid-off; no run.' That is the first type. 'He has gone right forward and driven that one past mid-off's left hand and the batsmen have taken two runs' is the second type. The first type corresponds to the stroke you will have used to hit those stationary balls in the fifth exercise, a forward defensive stroke with the bat inclined so as to keep the ball well down. The second type of offensive stroke is started in just the same way, but more power is put into the shot and consequently the bat has to follow after the ball. The details will be described under the heading of 'the drive', but first we will consider the easier scoring strokes which are played to short balls on the off or the leg.

To score from short balls on the off side

There are two ways of playing these strokes, and you should watch some good batsmen to see which they use and the circumstances when they use them. The two variations are just those of moving either your left foot or your right. The easier stroke is that with the left foot moved across, and it is the one usually used for slow or medium paced bowling; it is called the 'cut drive', and it is definitely the stroke to practice first.

When a player decides that a ball will pass at least a foot outside the off stump and that it is a short ball, he places his left foot across to the off side and at the same time lifts the bat *further* back, so that his hands are near the right shoulder. There is then a slight pause while the ball is allowed to come to the top of its flight. Then the bat swings out and slightly downwards with the object of driving the ball in the direction of cover-point. At the end of the stroke, the bat and the arms should all be in one line.

The motion for this stroke is that of driving a long pole at an angle of about 20 degrees into the ground. In fact, if you have an old bat, the stroke can be practised in that way. Get a long curtain rod and push it into a soft piece of ground at about 20 degrees from the horizontal, using a Y-shaped stick as a prop. Take up your stance so that the rod is directed as towards cover-point, lift up your bat in the usual way, move your left foot across and then, keeping your arm firm, drive the rod further into the ground by means of successive blows with your old

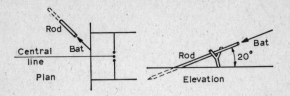

bat. The rod should, of course, be hit with the driving part of the bat.

The main points to note in this exercise are that the stroke has to be in a downward direction and that the bat should be allowed to remain in contact with the rod; when such a stroke is made at a ball, there will be no fear of giving a catch. For further practice, the ball hanging in its net at the appropriate height of 2 to 3 feet above the ground can be used. Only one bang at the ball can be had at a time! The cut proper, played by moving the *right* foot, will be described later. Good length balls on the off should be allowed to pass by without attempting a stroke, because the wicket-keeper and the slips are waiting for the catches given by such risky shots.

To score from balls on the leg side

Unless a bowler bowls leg-breaks, he is usually advised never to aim on the leg side; such advice assumes that the batsman will score off the majority of leg balls, and this *should* be the case. Most boys, however, are noticeably bad at playing on the leg side, unless the ball is a rank long hop or full toss. There are two reasons for this weakness: firstly, small boys dislike balls that are liable to hit them on the body if they miss them, and, secondly, if the ball is so wide that it is going to pass behind them, they make a sweep round in an attempt to make the bat catch up with the ball. In order to counteract these bad tendencies, try to remember these two tips. When a ball is bowled towards your body, do not move back but step forward on to the right foot as in the back stroke, and always aim to hit the ball in front of the square-leg umpire, not behind him.

For most balls on the leg side, you have only to modify the forward and back strokes already practised. When the ball is pitched well up, a forward stroke is naturally played, but the chief difficulty is to keep your left leg out of the way. Consequently, the left leg must be moved directly backwards and slightly to your left, so as to allow the bat to swing in front of the leg and so hit the ball in front of the square-leg umpire. The right foot pivots round slightly. The following diagrams explain this movement:

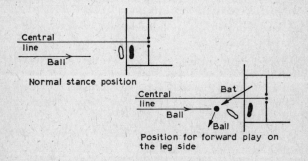

Normal stance position

Position for forward play on the leg side

It is much easier to give the above instructions than it is to carry them out, because a batsman becomes so accustomed to moving his left foot down the pitch towards the bowler that it requires considerable concentration to move it elsewhere. In fact, once you have moved your left foot wrongly, it is impossible to get the bat to meet the ball, and this is one common cause of half-volleys on the leg being missed. The stroke can be practised with a stationary ball which should be placed 10 to 14 inches in front of the left foot. For a good length ball on the leg side, the forward defensive shot can be played, with the object of pushing the ball about 10 yards away on the on side, and then, if there is no fielder at short-leg or silly mid-on, a short run can often be taken. For short balls on the leg, the stroke used depends on the direction of the ball, whether on your body or well behind it. For those actually on or just outside the leg stump, a back stroke is played, while for the wider balls a cross-bat stroke is used.

The back stroke or leg push

This is a most valuable stroke and one that will gain you many runs; it will come quite easily if you have learnt the normal back stroke in the proper way. It is the placing of your right foot forward and in front of the wicket that paves the way for the correct playing of all short balls on the leg side. The only modification that you have to make is to turn your left shoulder round towards mid-wicket and get your head as usual along the line of flight of the ball. The stroke with the bat is a push which should aim at guiding the ball in a direction away from any fielder. For fast balls it develops into a glide to long-leg.

The cross-bat stroke on the leg side

This stroke is a form of hook, but that name is usually applied to a more advanced stroke used for short balls on the wicket. Just as the back stroke cannot be played to balls wide of the off stump, so it is on the leg side. The arm movement is a natural swing of the bat across

the body, the stroke in this case being entirely con-
trolled by the right hand; it is, in fact, just the very
stroke which you have to avoid in the rest of your batting.
Once again, the important factor is the position of the
left leg; get it well across towards square-leg to give your
arms all the freedom they want. Bend both elbows,
so as to give the face of the bat a chance to hit the ball,
and aim *in front of square-leg*.

As in the case of all strokes, there is one point on
which to concentrate just as you are about to hit the ball,
and that is the height; many a promising innings has
come to an abrupt end by a catch on the leg side off a bad
short ball. The stroke should be made with the bat
swinging slightly downwards; or, in other words, the
ball should be hit in such a way that it bounces before
reaching a fielder alongside the square-leg umpire.
If, however, there are one or more fielders nearer than
that, you must aim to hit the ball up and over their
heads, if you consider that risk justifiable. It is all the
more essential, therefore, to keep in mind the position of
the leg-side fielders and to remember that they may move
when your back is turned! This cross-bat stroke is a
favourite one for left-handers and they very rarely miss;
they are, however, liable to drop their left shoulders and
so hit the ball too much in the air.

This sweep round to leg is not to be confused with the
so-called 'cow-shot' of the village green. Even though
the two strokes are almost identical in execution, the
correct one is played to a ball already outside the leg
stump, whereas the village blacksmith tries to bring it
off against balls consistently pitching well on the off side
of the wicket. Sometimes, of course, he succeeds, but
only as the result of perfect timing. All the same, it must
be admitted that the 'cow-shot' is often a very effective
method of attack for a No. 10 or No. 11 batsman against
a steady good length bowler.

Summary of Elementary Strokes

Type of Stroke	Type of ball for which it is used	Main point to keep in mind for the stroke
Back stroke	Slow balls of good length. All balls short of a good length	Move right forward so as to get your head on the line of the ball's flight
Forward defensive stroke	Fast balls of good length. Yorkers	See that your left foot is as near as possible to the pitch of the ball. If on the wicket, do not be late
Forward offensive stroke	Half-volleys. Full pitches	Get your head over the ball as it is hit, so as to avoid giving a catch
Cross-bat stroke on the off—'cut drive'	Short balls a foot or more outside off stump	Hit the ball down
Leg push	Short balls nearly on the leg stump	Move right foot to turn shoulders round
Cross-bat stroke on leg side	Short balls wide on the leg-side	Do not hit ball into fielders' hands

Applying the elementary strokes during actual play

So far, the movements of arms and feet required for the essential strokes have been described in some detail and individual practices have been suggested. Sooner or later you will have someone to bowl a moving ball to you, either in a net or in an actual game. It is one thing to go through the motions of a stroke without a ball and quite another to apply these movements successfully. A number of suggestions will therefore be made for this purpose. They can be classified under the functions of three important parts of our bodies not previously mentioned—the brain, the eyes and the wrists. As the brain works as a result of messages from the eyes, these two must be considered together.

Use of brain and eyes

The eyes are used in two stages: first, to interpret the type of ball that is coming to you as soon as possible after it leaves the bowler's hand and, second, to watch the ball hit by the bat. The eyes judge the place where the ball is likely to pitch by several means, but mainly by the height of the ball above the ground relative to its speed. When a ball rises higher than the point at which it left the bowler's hand, it will be expected to be at least a half-volley unless it is a very slow ball. As will be explained in the chapter on bowling, a bowler who can 'flight' a ball is able to deceive a batsman by producing a peculiar delivery which looks like being a half-volley but which, for some reason, drops quickly and falls short of that length. Such bowlers are, however, rare, so with experience and plenty of practice your eyes will seldom give you the wrong message. The brain takes this message and combines it with a number of other thoughts before controlling the muscles that move the arms and legs. These 'other thoughts' will be those usually given to you by other advisers; here are some examples in words:

'I am playing a fast bowler on a fast wicket; when in doubt I must play forward.'

'There are several fielders at short-leg; I will only hit a ball on the leg side so hard that there is no chance of it being caught by one of them.'

'I have been told to stay in; therefore I will take no risk.'

When you hear that phrase 'What a foolish stroke', it is usually the part played by the brain which is at fault. The actual execution of the stroke may have been perfect, but it was not suitable to the particular occasion. The correct mental working of the brain is generally referred to as 'experience', and there is nothing much that a beginner can do about it except to 'live and learn', just as we do in other walks of life.

The second action of the eyes is to *watch the ball on to the bat*. This instruction is given to all games played with a ball. Golfers, for instance, attribute most bad shots to 'head up', which means that at the moment of striking the ball, the head had moved up so that the eyes were no longer watching the ball. When you play tennis, do you see your racket actually hit the ball, or at that moment are you looking over the net at the place where you intend the ball to go? Now a cricket bat is much narrower than a racket and the ball may change its direction in the last few feet before reaching your bat; consequently, it is essential to *follow the ball all the way up to your bat*. Whatever you do, you must avoid the tendency to look up in the direction of the expected stroke.

The use of the wrists for timing the stroke

In all the instructions for arm movements, no mention was made of the wrists. They are a form of springy connection between the arms and the hands that grip the bat. Their use is often a natural one in other pursuits such as using a hammer, bowing a stringed instrument and using a billiard cue. If the wrists are kept stiff in those movements, the result is a very poor one. The main action of the wrist is to *accelerate* the moving hammer or cue more rapidly than is possible with the arm alone. When a ball is struck by a racket, cue or bat, there is a definite but very short period of time during which the ball remains in actual contact with the moving object. While this contact remains, it makes a great difference for the motion to accelerate, as distinct from moving at a steady velocity or slowing up. Thus a cricket ball hit by an accelerating bat flies off the bat at great speed, and such a stroke is generally described as being 'well timed'. The sensation of a really well-timed stroke is something which is not easily forgotten.

In a cricket stroke, the wrists are generally used as follows. The bat is lifted back at first by a bend of the wrists and then by the arms. For a high back lift when a scoring stroke is anticipated, the wrists usually bend again at the end of the back lift. On the downward movement, the arms move first and the wrists come into play just before the ball is hit, thus giving the bat that acceleration which has been mentioned above. The wrists are also able to correct to some extent errors in the timing of the arm movement. For instance, if the arms have brought the bat down too soon, then the wrist movement, by being slow, will delay the bat in the last stage before the ball arrives. In a similar way, if the arms are late, very quick wrist movement may get the bat there in time. In fact, the watching of the ball when it is within 2 yards of the bat and the use of the wrists during that period make all the difference between a first-class batsman and an ordinary one.

Watching a batsman in action

When you have had some experience in trying to play the essential strokes, then is the time to learn by watching others. If you are a spectator at a match, try to get as close as possible to your 'model player', preferably behind the nets when he is practising. If that is not possible, use a pair of binoculars. Next you must realize that you intend to learn something and that you are not just an interested spectator. The difference is this: while the general spectator follows the ball from start to finish, the keen pupil concentrates on observing the player and only sees the ball when it reaches the player. So, if you are using binoculars, focus them on the batsman; see him take his stance; watch him lift his bat, move his feet and play the stroke; do not worry about the ball. Notice such things as how far back he lifts the bat, which foot he moves first and whether he watches the ball on to the bat or not. Try to compare his movements with your own. One point most likely to come to your notice will be the fluent action of his stroke; nothing is jerky, nothing is hurried, yet, when required, the power is there.

Watching through films

There are available nowadays a number of films specially taken for instructional purposes. These pictures generally give the view that has already been recommended. The camera does not attempt to follow the ball all the way down the pitch, but usually remains pointed at the batsman, so that you see his movements from start to finish. Even in this case, however, it is better to concentrate on watching part of his body instead of getting a general impression. Here the film has a big advantage, because, if under your control, it can be repeated as often as required; so that for the first run-through you can watch the batsman's feet, the second time his head and shoulders in relation to the moving bat, and so on. As will also be mentioned in the chapter on bowling, any slow motion pictures will show you how the movements of various parts of the body take place one after the other, starting from an unexpected quarter as often as not. For example, a forward stroke can be seen to start not by a movement of the bat but by a movement of the upper left arm, followed by the left elbow, and so on.

While we are on this subject, another good tip is to collect photographs and news-cuttings of famous batsmen in action, not just for the collecting habit but rather to develop a critical faculty. Schoolboys who are really keen on cricket can teach themselves a lot about the art of batting by studying such photographs and carefully analysing a particular stroke. For instance, a collection of off-drives by a dozen different batsmen would be not merely interesting but very instructive; and there are plenty of opportunities to obtain such a collection during the summer months from the daily and weekly papers and magazines. An album of such action photographs, neatly arranged and mounted, would prove to be much more than a hobby to its creator.

More strokes to learn

When you have watched good batsmen either on the field or in films, you will have found that they use many more strokes than you have so far been advised to learn. But it is best to start with the fundamental ones and get those more or less correct before trying more difficult or risky shots. Three of these latter will now be described: the forward drive (including use of the feet to move down the pitch), the cut and the hook.

1. *The forward drive*
This is an extension of the forward stroke already learnt. The bat is lifted farther back and is allowed to follow through after the ball. The tip of the bat, in fact, moves nearly in a complete circle, rather like the head of a golf

club. For the back lift, both elbows are bent and at the same time the wrists turn, so that the blade of the bat faces point. Note that this is different from the lift for the defensive forward stroke. The body should not be bent and the shoulder should remain pointing down the wicket. The leg movements are the same as for the forward stroke previously described. For a ball well on the off, that is suitable for a cover drive, the right foot

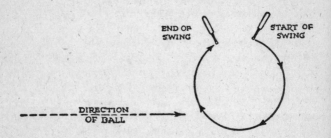

must pivot round on the toe so that the shoulders point in the direction of extra cover. The bat should be swung down and through, along the line which the ball is going to take; the hands and arms also go after the ball and thus *away* from the body. The left shoulder and hip must not swing round (as they do in a golf swing) but must remain firm, allowing the arms to move freely after the ball and all the weight to come on to the left leg. The wrists must not turn the bat round, but the left hand must keep the blade facing first the ball and then up to the sky. One final instruction: watch the bat hit the ball and do not look up after the stroke.

Moving out to drive. If a ball is about to pitch just short of a half-volley, it can be made into a half-volley by moving the feet quickly to take you a yard or so out of your crease. It is a stroke particularly suited for playing slow bowling of good length. A common mistake is to think of it as 'jumping out of your crease'; the movement is rather a swift sideways glide. A long stride down the pitch is taken by the left foot, and the right foot is moved up behind the left foot so that the feet are crossed over. The weight is then transferred to this right foot, and from there you play the normal drive. You should be about 2 feet from your original stance. It is hardly necessary to say that at all costs you must not miss the ball! When, therefore, you move out to play such a ball on the off side, remember to move not only down the pitch but also across to the off. Remember, too, that the ball is usually missed by playing *inside* it. While you are moving, keep the upper part of your body, and especially your head, quite steady; that is one reason for avoiding any form of upward jump. As will be mentioned later, the foot movement described is valuable not only for a drive but also for a defensive forward stroke. Also, by the time you have moved out of your crease, you may realize that you are not going to make the ball a half-volley after all, so that a drive will only send it into the air; you must then alter your intended drive into a quiet forward stroke.

2. *The Cut*

As previously indicated, this term is kept for a cross-bat stroke played with the right foot moved across the wicket, the ball usually being placed behind point. A 'square cut' will usually travel past point's left hand down towards third man, while a 'late cut' will run along the ground past where a second slip would normally be fielding. The stroke is not an easy one, since it requires perfect timing. For that reason, until you have 'played yourself in', that is become quite used to the pace of the wicket, this cut stroke should not be attempted; in that case, either let the ball pass by or else play a normal back stroke. It is a stroke, however, which should be practised frequently in net play, whenever you can persuade someone to bowl you suitable balls. These should be medium-fast short balls, well on the off. If a bowler cannot produce these to order, a friend could throw the same type of ball as if he were throwing a long hop to the wicket.

The technique is as follows. Lift the bat well up as for the drive, move the right leg back towards the wicket and across to the off—in other words, towards second slip— and point the right toe in the direction desired to hit the ball. Then wait until the ball is almost past you and bring the arms smartly down, aiming to catch the ball well up the bat. In fact, many players have been helped to master this stroke by being advised to get their hands nearly in contact with the ball. The cut is one of those strokes which you are more likely to learn by copying others or by studying a slow motion film than by any description in writing. Some beginners imagine that they are cutting balls by playing a vertical bat inclined at such an angle that a ball will be deflected or sliced off the bat in the direction of third man; such a stroke, however, is never used intentionally by good players. Once a batsman is really set and seeing the ball well, the cut makes an excellent foil to the drive when playing fast-medium bowling. With a flick of the wrists, a short ball is cut downwards through the slips; the bowler throws his next ball deliberately further up the pitch and the batsman drives him smartly through the covers; the next delivery is shorter and is cut again; and so on. All the same, the cut is not an easy stroke to learn, and beginners are advised to be cautious in its use.

3. *The hook or pull*
The hook is a stroke which requires a specially quick reaction and definite courage on the part of the batsman,

particularly when played to a ball of medium or fast pace. It is especially suitable to faster balls that pitch short of a length, because, even if such a ball is straight and is missed, it will usually pass well over the top of the stumps. The great danger in using the hook is not the missing of the ball altogether but the mishit off the edge of the bat which will tend to sky the ball. For this reason, the stroke should never be attempted until the batsman is well set and able to judge the pace of the wicket.

As soon as you spot that a ball is short and capable of being hooked, the bat is lifted not straight back over the stumps but out towards third man. At the same time, the right foot is placed about 6 inches forward to take all the weight of the body, while the left foot is moved back, as shown in the figure. This brings the shoulders almost right across the line of the wickets, and the eye should be right behind the line of the on-coming ball. It is essential to realize that if you miss the ball, it is going to hit you, probably on the chest or abdomen. If, however, you move into the right position quickly, you can then sweep

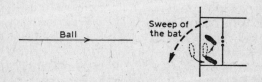

the bat across in front of you at the estimated height and there will be little fear of missing the ball completely. As mentioned above, if 'your eye is not in', you will probably fail to get the ball in the middle of the bat or else you will mistime it and so be liable to give an easy catch. On the other hand, when you have played yourself in,

the satisfaction of hitting the ball firmly in the middle of
the bat and steering it to the boundary away from any
fielders is worth all the practice that you should put in to
learn this stroke.

The sweep of the bat is just the same as for a leg stroke
to a short ball, and the same precautions have to be
taken to avoid being caught. It is said that such a great
batsman as Sutcliffe was occasionally trapped by the
Australians in this way; they posted a fielder on the
square-leg boundary and the bowler would send down
the necessary tempting long hop. One of the finest
hookers of all time was Patsy Hendren; and any reader
who can still remember the agility of that grand batsman
as he punched away to leg any fast bowler who dared
to pitch one short of a length will have seen the perfect
model.

Batting tactics

The fascination of cricket lies in its 'glorious uncertainty',
in the rapid fluctuations of fortune that are possible. The
score at one moment may be 100 for no wicket; ten
minutes later, it may be 105 for four; then, an hour later,
it may be 200 and still only four wickets down. In other
words, a batting side may hold the initiative with their
batsmen well on top of the bowling and then, in one
short disastrous over, they may suddenly lose that
initiative to the fielding side. The aim, or tactics, of a side
should be to gain the upper hand and then to keep it.
For a batting side, this means that the batsmen must
keep on attacking the bowling, punishing all loose balls
while treating all good balls on their merits. But once the
batsmen fall back on the defensive, the fielders will move
in and be right on their toes to snap up catches from the
timid strokes that are played.

As these various situations occur in a game, the players

have to adapt their normal game to their captain's requirements. Let us first consider the stages of a typical innings under normal conditions and then discuss the variations which may be required. When you have taken your guard, have a good look at the positions of all the fielders, especially those on the leg side. Then decide in what direction you can best place the ball for a single. If some of the fielders stand unpleasantly close to you, make up your mind that *either* you will not hit a ball in their direction *or* that you will try to hit so hard that they will think it wiser to retreat a few yards. Now comes the stage of 'playing yourself in'. Even if you are sent in to score rapidly, it always pays to play yourself in, although if you are given the alternative of scoring quickly or getting out this playing-in stage will have to be a short one. Normally, it is at least two or three overs, depending, of course, on how much of the bowling you receive.

It has already been stated that in batting the eyes, the brain and the muscles work together in a wonderful way and have to do this work in a very short time. 'Playing-in' means getting that co-ordination going. The eyes have to accustom themselves to the light, the brain has to interpret the pace of the bowling, and the muscles have to move the bat and body in the way the brain decides. You must also get used to the exact pace at which the ball comes off the pitch. During this process, your main object is to *watch the ball* right on to the bat. If the bowler bowls short enough for you to play back, your job is made much easier; that is why you hear it sometimes said that Blank's bowling just 'plays the batsmen in'. Do not, at this early stage, lift up your bat so far as you will do later on, and be content to play most balls quietly. Yet if the bowler gives you a loose one, by all means help yourself to some runs. It is a good tip, when you are at the bowler's end, to study his methods at close range—how he spins the balls, how he varies his tactics and how he changes his action for different balls. In the case of a slow bowler especially, you can often benefit considerably by watching such things carefully.

Once you have made your first dozen or twenty runs, your scoring strokes can gradually become a little more free, but do not be content with your moderate score. Then is the time to concentrate on making another twenty, and so on. Far too many young players make scores of twenty but not more. Yet the acceleration can be considerable, and you will generally find that a good player scores the second half of a century twice as fast as the first fifty.

So much, then, for a standard innings; but one of the fascinating features of cricket is that the state of the game often demands exceptions from that standard. Firstly, there is the happy position of a side which wants runs quickly and can well afford to lose several wickets in the process. If this occurs when your side requires a certain number of runs to win in a limited number of minutes, it always pays the batsmen—or the captain— to do a little mental arithmetic. Let us suppose you want 60 runs to win and have only 40 minutes left for play; that means $1\frac{1}{2}$ runs per minute. Now an average over takes $3\frac{3}{4}$ minutes, or 16 to the hour; therefore, if you and your partner make 6 runs an over between you, your side will be just 'in front of the clock'. So try to keep up that average; but remember that often the rate of scoring will be slowed down if you get out, at any rate until the next batsman has played himself in. On the other hand, if you cannot keep up to the four runs per over standard, it is better for one of you to get out and let the next batsman have a try.

If you have been set to score as many runs as possible in, say, the next three overs before the innings is to be

declared closed, do not try to hit the very first ball for
six. Play the first few balls on their merits and then, if
the bowling keeps to a good length, you must use your
feet, either to make half-volleys by running out or else to
step right back for pulls or cuts according to your pre-
ference. If your partner can score quicker than you, try
to give him all the bowling, and when you are the
striker do your best to score a single at the *beginning* of
each over, while refraining from taking an odd number
of runs off the *last* ball. Remember, too, that four quick
singles in succession are sometimes more valuable than
one boundary, because they tend to rattle the fielding
side.

Last-wicket partnerships

The tactics of a No. 10 or No. 11 when batting with a
player who is well set and who can go on making any
number of runs provided his partner does not get out are
of special interest. The run-getter should be responsible
for all the calling at the expense of the normal rules.
While batting, he should only score by means of twos,
fours or sixes until the end of the over approaches; then
comes the real fun. The fielding side will naturally do
all they can to stop that precious single being taken
from the fifth or sixth ball, and it is then vitally urgent
that his partner should back up well, nearly half-way
down the pitch if necessary. Now and again our No. 11
will have to play the bowling, of course. If it is towards
the end of an over, he should attempt nothing except
the defence of his wicket; but if he has to face the bowling at the beginning of an over, he will naturally try to
steal a quick single.

The main stroke for 'keeping your end up' is a *prod* at
the ball, with the head well over the ball to keep it down.
Do not even try to hit a tempting ball. There is a story

that Herbert Sutcliffe once had a bet with Wilfred Rhodes that he would play an over blindfolded against Rhodes' bowling without being bowled. Sutcliffe, who was allowed to take guard, merely left his bat upright covering nearly all the wicket and Rhodes failed to get any of the six balls past the bat to hit the stumps. It matters little whether that story is true or not; the point is that if a batsman takes a 'centre' guard and remains quite static with his bat held vertically in the block, it is extremely difficult to bowl him out. The result is that these last-wicket partnerships, with one man doing all the scoring, can be great fun—at least for the batting side and their supporters!

'Nursing' the bowling

Somewhat similar tactics can be applied with advantage during the ordinary part of an innings when the two bowlers are well contrasted; one may be fast and the other slow. Now an experienced or well-set batsman can often shield a new partner from the particular bowler who is likely to trouble him most. In the days when Grimmett used to worry many an England batsman, a left-hander, such as Leyland, would arrange to play most of Grimmett's bowling, leaving a right-hander to play the other end. The better players in school sides might well copy this idea to help their less experienced fellows in the early stages of their innings. Remember, in fact, that batting is done by partnerships, not by a number of individuals.

Playing for a draw

Finally, there are the rather grim tactics to avoid defeat by making the result a draw. The phrase 'playing for a draw' rather implies that this was the only object of the game and that the incentive of a win was never present. Rather let us imagine that a side has been left with 200 runs to win in two hours; the earlier batsmen make 90 for four in the first hour, but in an attempt to force the pace the score is now 130 for seven, with only 35 minutes left for play. The captain of the batting side regards two runs per minute as being beyond the capabilities of his last few batsmen and accordingly instructs them to play for a draw. If you are one of those batsmen, it is best to play more or less your normal game, but do not take any risks. There is no point, for instance, in running any short runs. Yet it is important to remember that a maiden over takes only two minutes to deliver, whereas one in which six singles are scored may take three or more minutes. In fact, every run scored is nearly equivalent to another ball safely played. For that reason, do not place yourself *unduly* on the defensive but take all the safe runs that you can. If a side can rely on its tail-end batsmen playing out time, the earlier players can bat more freely and so make the game much brighter.

Summary of batting strokes

Now that a detailed description of the more common batting strokes has been given, they can best be summarized by means of an approximate diagram.

In addition to the strokes shown in the following diagram, there will, of course, be many short 'pushes', varying in distance from 5 to 15 yards from the batsman. Runs may or may not be taken from these semi-defensive push strokes according to the state of the game and the positions of the opposing fielders. When the leg glide becomes an extremely delicate stroke, it is sometimes called a 'glance'.

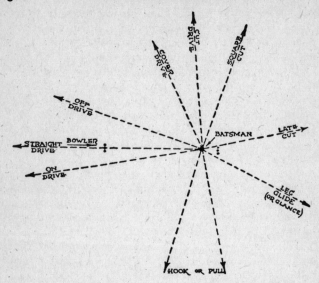

Batting against bowling of various speeds

Even first-class batsmen have their preferences for playing fast or slow bowling, so it is only to be expected that anyone beginning to learn the game may develop a liking for one type and a dislike for another. There are also the natural reasons for such variations. The tall player, for example, with his long reach, will be more likely to play fast bowling on a good wicket with ease, because his reach will enable him to play any ball pitched reasonably well up by making it into a half-volley. In addition, if he also possesses good wrists, he will be able to cut or glide short balls on the off or leg sides respectively. The shorter player, unless he is adept at the pull, will be at a disadvantage. On the other hand, any batsman who is quick on his feet will be better qualified to play slow bowling. Assuming, then, that we all have our likes and dislikes, it is our job to try to obtain as much net practice as possible against bowling of the type we dislike; in addition, we can apply some of the advice which follows.

1. *Playing slow bowling*

The difficulty of batting against slow bowling varies enormously according to the state of the wicket. A slow, soft wicket will allow the ball to turn considerably, but it will only come slowly off the pitch; therefore, by playing back to most balls, the break can be seen, provided that the ball is watched right on to the bat. On a slow wicket, the most difficult slow ball to play is really the one which is just short of a half-volley, because, even in the few inches which the ball travels after hitting the ground until it reaches the bat, the change in direction may be such as to meet the edge of the bat instead of the middle. The one essential for playing slow bowling is the use of the feet in order to move out of your crease and make the ball into a full pitch.

The method of moving the feet one behind the other has been described for the forward drive; just the same movement is used, but it is not necessary to drive the slow ball when you have gone out to meet it. You may find at the last moment that you have miscalculated its length and that, instead of a full pitch, you have made it into a yorker; in that case, a quiet stroke should be played. Remember, however, that once you have left your crease you *must* hit the ball, even if it is only a yard or two. Nevertheless, every time you can go out and make a full pitch, you should be able to drive it to the appropriate place. If you cannot make a full pitch, then by playing back you should find enough time for a normal backstroke. As soon as the bowler drops one at all short, a pull or a square cut or a drive through the covers should be easy. For these reasons, a slow bowler on a slow wicket has to keep a very good length to prevent you from scoring quite easy runs, especially if you are prepared to use your feet to move down the wicket, and provided that your judgment is quick and sound.

Slow bowling on a *hard* wicket is slightly different. If the wicket has not worn, the ball will not change its direction more than an inch or two in a yard movement forward. On the other hand, it will come off the wicket much faster. A well-pitched-up ball is therefore not such a dangerous one, but a good length ball, if left as such, will probably bowl you if it turns a few inches on to the line of the wicket. In this case, do not play back to good length balls, but more out so as to make them half-volleys which can probably be driven safely along the ground.

Finally, we come to the slow bowler's paradise, the 'sticky wicket' or the 'worn patch'. The batsman is now really in a tight corner, because the ball will not only turn but turn quickly. Nothing has been said so far about an important preliminary to good batsmanship—observing which way the ball is going to turn. This should always be done by watching the bowler's hand. Generally speaking, if the ball comes from the *front* of the bowler's hand it will be an off-break from a right-arm bowler and a leg-break from a left-arm bowler. If the ball comes out of the *back* of the bowler's hand, it will usually be the opposite kind of break. Now on a difficult wicket, it is absolutely vital to know which break is to be expected, even if on easier wickets it is not quite so essential. As before, you should move out to smother this break, but again you must be careful about balls which are nearly half-volleys or you will probably edge them on one side or the other. When you are compelled to play back, make as much use as possible of your pads as a second line of defence, bearing in mind the l.b.w. rules, of course. This is an appropriate place to explain those rules from the batsman's point of view.

If the ball pitches outside the leg stump, according to the present rules you cannot be given out l.b.w. You can therefore afford to play back to any such ball with your legs in between the pitch of the ball and the wicket. If an off-breaking ball pitches outside the off stump, you will not be out l.b.w. if you move your legs *beyond* the line of the off stump. It is a valuable exercise to practise playing back with the legs moving in both these ways. The use of the mirror is again excellent for this practice, especially with two parallel lines marked on the floor to give the line of the wickets, as in the diagram below:

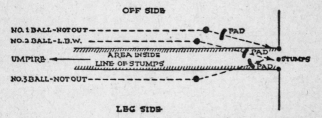

In the three cases shown above, ball No. 1 could be stopped by your pad without your being l.b.w. because the point of impact is outside the line of the off stump, even though the ball would have hit the wicket. Ball No. 2 will certainly get you l.b.w., whereas ball No. 3, being pitched outside the leg stump, would require a 'not out' decision from the umpire.

A slow bowler usually has to place a majority of his fielders on one side of the wicket, as well as one or more in the deep field. It follows that there must be some gaps on the other side, and as a batsman you should always be on the look out for a chance to place the ball into those gaps. It is much better to score by frequent singles than by an occasional boundary followed by a number of misses; in the former case, the bowler and his fielders tend to become discouraged, while in the latter they develop a more 'offensive' spirit. The batsman's best chance, then, against the slow bowler on his sticky wicket, is to smother all balls pitched up at good length or beyond and to drive any ball which can be made into a full pitch. Also, when you play back, be careful to observe the type of break and use your pads behind your bat, placing the ball where you can take a single if possible. And, finally, remember that twenty runs made under those conditions are worth fifty or more on an easy wicket.

2. *Playing fast bowling*

There is always a tendency for young players to dislike or fear fast bowling. It is true that when you stop a fast ball on some unprotected part of your body it is more painful than the stopping of a slow ball; but that is not the real reason, since few players mind taking some hard knocks at any game. The main reason is lack of experience in playing fast bowling, because for every good fast bowler in most cricket sides there will be five or six medium or slow ones. If you can once obtain some confidence in the playing of fast balls on a good wicket, you will generally be disappointed when such a bowler is taken off. That was certainly the case when Grimmett and O'Reilly played for the Australians. When the opening fast bowlers were on, the England batting almost invariably looked good, but as soon as the shine was off the ball and Bradman called on his spin bowlers, the batsmen suddenly seemed second-class. For that reason, then, you should try to persuade a friend who can deliver the ball fairly fast to bowl to you on a good wicket, or, failing that, on concrete covered by a mat. It is only such practice which can bring confidence.

The first point to realize about fast bowling is that,

unless the ball is pitched up nearly as far as a half-volley, the ball will go over the top of your wicket. It follows that, provided you go forward to meet the ball, it should be difficult for a fast bowler to hit the stumps; in fact, as you will read in the chapter on bowling, much of the attack of a fast bowler is made by balls which are not intended to hit the wickets. The main danger, of course, is at the beginning of your innings, before you have got your eyes accustomed to follow a fast ball. For this reason, do not attempt too much in the way of scoring shots until you have become used to the pace of the wicket; also, it is best not to lift the bat back as far as usual. Another good tip is to aim at meeting the ball with a firm stroke, gripping the bat a little more tensely at the moment of impact.

It is much harder to time the stroke accurately if you use a long swing of the bat, and most players are bowled as a result of bringing down the bat too late. This was particularly the case in the Fifth Test Match at the Oval in August 1948, when the Australian fast bowler, Lindwall, was mainly responsible for England's feeble batting display. Every now and then Lindwall unleashed his fastest possible ball, and each time the England batsmen brought down their bats too late. In several cases one could actually see them making quite a reasonable stroke a fraction of a second after the ball had passed the bat! Yet if only those same batsmen had been able to survive their first few overs, the probability is that they would have settled down to play Lindwall like any other fast bowler.

On the whole, it is best to be ready to play forward by having little weight on the left foot, so that you can move it immediately you have made a decision. If the fast bowler has a new ball, as is usually the case for the opening bowlers, the new ball is liable to swerve and must be watched with great care, both while you are the striker and while you are at the other end. For out-swingers, that is balls starting on the wicket and swerving away to the off, make a rule for yourself that, whenever they are pitched up and not going to hit the wicket, you will let the ball pass by, at any rate in the early stages of your innings. If you avoid getting out in those two common ways—playing late and touching an out-swinger—and if you have acquired a few scoring strokes, you should get plenty of runs.

In playing fast balls, the batsman has the advantage that he need not swing the bat fast or hit the ball hard to make it reach the boundary; the ball already has pace and it only requires guiding away from the fielders. Every short ball more than a foot outside the off stump should be cut behind point, probably for four runs; every ball pitched up but on the leg side should be glided off the bat to fine-leg; and, once you have played yourself in to the pace of the wicket and the bowler, every half-volley can be driven back hard enough to beat most fielders, unless you send the ball directly to them. The batsman usually has another advantage in that the wicket-keeper stands back for fast bowling, and you can therefore move forward out of your crease to meet the ball without the fear of being stumped.

To sum up, then, a fast bowler has the advantage over the batsman for the first few overs that he bowls, because the batsman is not accustomed to the pace and his general rate of reaction is liable to be too slow; but once that period is over, the advantage should then lie with the batsman.

CHAPTER 4

Running Between the Wickets

Since it is the batsman's prime object to obtain as many runs as possible, the actual running of them is almost as important as the strokes which guide the ball past the fielders. Of course, if you are in the happy position of being able to raise your score by a series of fours and sixes, any running is unnecessary; but this only happens rarely, and certainly not at the start of an innings. Good running between the wickets is a pleasure to watch and an equal pleasure to take part in, although it involves vigorous exercise. It can be summed up as the art of obtaining every run that is possible without taking an unnecessary risk, and certainly without getting run out. If you watch school or club cricket, you may often find that a pair of batsmen can get the fielding side quite rattled by their running between the wickets.

The sequence of events often follows this kind of pattern. One of the batsmen manages to get the ball several times past the fielders when they are in their normal positions close to the wicket. This has the effect of making all the fielders drop back a few yards. The batsman then plays a quiet shot and calls for a short run; as the run is safely completed, a wild throw comes out of reach of the wicket-keeper and goes for a boundary overthrow, so that that quiet stroke counts five. The unfortunate fielder is then reprimanded by his captain and ordered to field closer in. The striker, however, places the next ball to another fielder some distance out, and he sends quite an accurate but particularly fast return to the bowler, who has the choice of either allowing another four runs to come from an overthrow or of having his hands damaged by stopping the ball, an unpleasant alternative. The field is now closed in again by the captain; but the bowler, with little feeling in his hand after stopping that hard return, bowls some loose balls, so that it is quite easy to place the ball past the fielders to the boundary. Thus, in the course of perhaps only a single over, the fielding side has quite lost control of the game, at least for the time being.

Such a pair of run-getters as those outlined above will have acquired a technique based on a number of fundamental principles. The first point to note is that, although a cricket pitch is 22 yards long, it is only necessary to run about 17 yards for each run scored. This is because the batting creases are each 4 feet in front of the stumps, and also because each batsman can pull up about another 4 feet short of the crease and reach the rest of the distance with the bat, the hand being extended to a full arm's length. If you are at the bowler's end, you should 'back up' for every ball. Do not start level with or behind the stumps and then move with the bowler as he finishes his run, because this is often disconcerting to the bowler and is a waste of energy in any case. The best position is to stand just outside the crease, with your bat resting on the ground inside the line, and then, as soon as the ball has left the bowler's hand, walk quite 2 or 3 yards down the pitch. Always remember that your partner may drive a ball straight back at your stumps and that the bowler may just get a hand to it; in that case, if you have not jumped back and placed your bat over the crease again, you are 'run out'. Provided, then, that you can pop your bat back in time in such an event, you should go as far down the wicket as possible, so that, if the ball goes behind the wicket and it is your call, it should be an easy run to the other end.

It is, however, the turning at each end when running more than a single over which boys and learners waste time. Never run as far as the other crease, and certainly not beyond it, unless you are making a great effort to avoid being run out. When you are within reach of the crease, stop your leg movement and prepare to turn for the run back; at the same time, touch the ground with the bat over—not on—the line. If both players run in this way, and run fast, they will make four runs under circumstances when most players would only obtain three. Contrariwise, only one run is often obtained when there should have been two, because one or both of two useful precepts have probably been ignored. These are, firstly, always run the first run as fast as possible and, secondly, never run past the wicket but turn in preparation for a possible second run. In such a way, advantage can be taken of any slight mistakes by the fielders, and the call for the second run can then be made.

One great failing with most young players is that they only run at half pace, as if they were on a long distance race instead of a 17-yard burst; lively running brightens up a game enormously, but do not forget to run your bat along the ground in front of you as you approach the crease or if there is the slightest chance of your being run out. In order not to damage the actual pitch, always run well to the side of it.

Calling for runs

The conventions for calling are fairly straightforward:

1. It is the striker's call when he hits the ball in front of him.
2. The correct words for the call are 'Yes' or 'No' or 'Wait'. In the case of 'wait', it should be followed as soon as possible by 'yes' or 'no'.

3. Once a call has been made, it should not be changed without careful consideration; W. G. Grace laid it down that, after a 'no' call, a batsman could change his mind and call 'yes' if there was at least a run and a half.

Of every five players run out, four are due to disregard of these three rules and only one as a result of brilliant fielding.

It is important to have the correct interpretation of the phrase 'in front of the striker'. The line AB in the diagram below is the best dividing line, which means

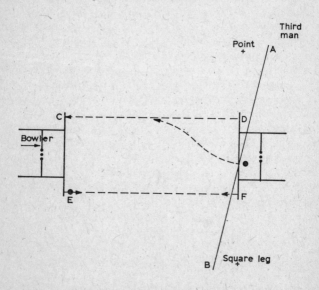

that the non-striker calls when the ball is hit to square-leg but that the striker himself calls when he hits the ball just behind point. It will be obvious that the striker will not see many balls which he hits towards square-leg, so that his partner should call them. There are two reasons why it is best for the striker to call for a stroke in the direction of A. Firstly, he can judge much better than his partner whether a ball is going past a fielder at point and, secondly, the stroke may be played with his weight on his back foot so that he will not be able to make a quick start for his run.

The diagram also shows the correct positions for the two batsmen as they run between the wickets. The striker should move to his off side and run to and fro along the line CD while his partner runs along the line EF. In this way, the chances of a collision are avoided. If the bowler delivers the ball from *round* the wicket, the positions are generally reversed, with the striker moving to his leg side.

In order to take advantage of scoring all the short runs possible, a simple quick call must be made. 'Come' is an alternative to 'yes'; but when one player says 'what about it?' and the other answers 'I think we can', the run could obviously have been completed by the time such conversations take place. The call, then, should be quick, loud and distinct, with an emphasis on the 's' of 'yes'. Remember that your voice has to carry nearly 20 yards to your partner even though there may be other distracting noises, such as a wind blowing, or the movement of the wicket-keeper, or possibly an appeal for l.b.w. when a leg bye may be obtained. Your call must be heard above all that.

Whenever you hit the ball hard in front of the wicket and it is going within reach of a fielder, it is best to call 'wait'. Such a call should produce an automatic reaction on the part of both players. They should each advance a few yards up the pitch so that if the fielder does not stop the ball cleanly the caller can say 'yes' and the run be completed; if, however, a smart piece of fielding sends the ball quickly back, either batsman should be able to return safely to his crease. Too often, though, when the call of 'wait' is made, the two players merely stand still, each one in his own crease, so that, even if a fumble is made by the fieldsman, there is not time to obtain a run. On the call 'wait', therefore, both batsmen should back up as far as possible.

So much for the initial call; next comes the question of who should call for the second and subsequent runs. In that case, the general rule is that the call is made by the player who has to reach the end of which the ball is more likely to be returned. As the players cross during their first run, the one who is facing the direction of the ball should help his partner, who should run hard without looking round. Let us take a common example. The striker makes an unexpected snick to leg and his partner calls him for a run; he sprints hard for the other end of the pitch but he has no idea whether there is one or several runs to be had, yet, as he will have to return to his original end for the second run, it will be his call. The non-striker who called for the first run can see exactly what is happening to the ball as he runs towards the wicket-keeper's end, and he should therefore try to judge the chances of a second run. So as the two players cross in the middle of the pitch, he might say 'two for that', or 'a possible three', or 'that's all' if he sees the ball already being returned.

Before we leave this important matter of calling and understanding between the batsmen, here are a few general guiding principles on the question of when a run should or should not be called:

1. Never call for a run from a direct hit to mid-off, mid-on or cover-point without saying 'wait'.

2. Always run for a hit to extra cover and to third man, unless he is very close in.

3. Always run 'one for the throw' when a fielder is out somewhere near the boundary.

4. Remember that it is much easier to obtain short quick singles when the ground is soft than when it is hard and the ball travels rapidly to the fielders. Thus the difficulty of scoring boundaries on soft wet grounds should be partly compensated by a number of well-placed singles.

5. Never risk running a single off a wide or a no ball; they count one in the scorebook anyhow.

6. 'Always run a catch' is a bad slogan. Quite often when a catch is missed the fielder, hoping to make up for his failure, throws the ball in hard and the striker is run out. So run a catch on its merits. If the ball is going in the air to extra-cover, run; but it it is going to mid-off, do not run unless it is a skier.

7. Remember that the standard of fielding improves as you move up into better-class games. The rules given above apply to almost all classes of cricket; but all players are liable to become accustomed to one standard of fielding so that they are likely to make mistakes when they change to another. As an example, a boy of sixteen who is a good runner will probably take a number of liberties when playing with boys of his own age; for instance, he may find that he can frequently steal a run when the ball goes to cover-point. Then, during the holidays, he is given a game for his local club where the standard of fielding is much quicker all round. He duly hits a ball to cover-point, calls 'yes', and runs out his partner, who may be one of the batting stars of the club. So he has to pay a hard price for his error of judgment and for his failure to adapt himself to his new environment. By all means take risks in practice games to see what runs you can steal, but do not take those same risks in matches or among strangers.

8. Finally, once a call has been made, do not change it. Never say 'yes—no' or 'no—yes'. Once you have started on a run and you are nearly half-way down the pitch, there is a far better chance if you carry on than if you stop, turn and go back. So, even if a brilliant piece of fielding follows your call of 'yes', be wary about changing your mind. Similarly, if a fumble follows your call of 'no', do not change it to 'yes'; remember that, once your partner who has been backing up hears 'no', he sets off back to his crease, and he will then be 'on the wrong foot' for starting a run. It is only when a fieldsman comletely misses a ball which you had expected him to stop that, with the agreement of your partner, an original 'no' can be altered to a decision in favour of a run.

Refusing a call

A few words will now be said on the question of reversing your partner's call and sending him back when he has called for a run. A batsman, especially if he is inexperienced or nervous, may make an obviously foolish call for a run; if his partner—as he should do—realizes this at once, it is his duty to call out immediately 'no—go back!' and the throwing away of a wicket may be avoided. Such a contradiction must be made before either player has moved more than 3 or 4 yards out of his crease. There are occasions, too, when a batsman who is well set has the right to send back a partner who has only made a few runs, even if it is fairly certain that the newcomer will be run out; if one of them has to go, it is far better for the less important player to be sacrificed. The policy of one player deliberately keeping the bowling, even though he has to refuse a few of his partner's calls, has been discussed in the section on batting tactics.

Exceptions to the generally accepted rules for running

It can be fairly said that any cricketer who does not conform to all the above principles is liable to be a menace to his side; he may give to the opposing team that particular wicket which none of their bowlers can obtain. In the chapter on watching cricket, you are warned not to imitate *everything* which first-class players do, and a special warning about some of the ideas you may pick up from their running and calling should be given here. Firstly, you may never hear a call of 'yes' or 'no'; that is probably because you are too far away to hear. You may actually see them beckon with the finger to each other. You will not find that this is a general practice; at the same time, there are a few cases where a run can be stolen from a fielder who has to turn round to go a few yards for the ball and so is unable to see what the batsmen are doing. Thinking that they are not running, he will take his time in recovering and returning the ball, and it would obviously be fatal if one of the batsmen suddenly shouted 'come on, then'. It is at such a time that a quiet signal is justified.

Another thing you are certain to notice in first-class cricket will be that a number of batsmen frequently walk the latter part of a run, a fact which seems a contradiction to the principle of running hard. In that connection, you must remember that an experienced player knows exactly when and where he can conserve his strength and also that a match lasting two or three or more days is quite a different type of cricket from a schoolboy's afternoon game. When Bradman batted for six hours in a day while the score was advanced by perhaps 400 runs—100 of which might have been boundaries—he obviously could not run 300 times up and down the wicket, that is about 3 miles, at top speed all the time. You will notice, however, that when an experienced batsman hits the ball past the bowler to a fielder in the deep he will start walking as soon as he realizes the fieldsman is going to return the ball in plenty of time to prevent a second run. But when the same batsman places the ball just wide of a fielder he will be off like a shot and down to the other end probably before you have discovered where the ball actually went.

This matter of running between the wickets is something which requires no specific skill; it merely demands alertness, keenness and experience built on sound principles. Your ability as a batsman can be improved considerably by good running, and the whole game can be made alive or dead by the corresponding attitude of the players. Let us all, therefore, learn to call 'yes', 'no' or 'wait' distinctly, and not alter our minds; to run the first run as hard as possible; not to run past the wickets but to run our bats along the ground when there is any danger of being run out; to back up well and sensibly; and to be always on our toes and on the look out for runs.

CHAPTER 5

Bowling

The first and almost the only object of a bowler is to get the batsman out. This, as a glance at the rules will show, can be done in five different ways:

1. The ball may evade the bat of the striker and hit the wicket so as to dislodge a bail—bowled.

2. The ball may evade the bat of the striker and, without hitting the wicket, draw him out from behind the crease, while the wicket-keeper gathers the ball and dislodges a bail with the ball in his hand—stumped.

3. The ball may meet the bat of the striker in such a way that it travels, without touching the ground, into the hands of the bowler or any other member of the fielding side and stays there—caught.

4. The ball, under certain conditions, may cause the striker to interpose his body between the ball and the wicket in such a way as to prevent it hitting the wicket—l.b.w.

5. The ball may cause the striker to move in such a way that, with his person or his bat, he dislodges a bail—hit wicket.

The batsman has two objectives. Firstly, he must make runs and, secondly, in order to be able to do that, he must avoid losing his wicket. So we can see that cricket is really a battle between the bowler and the batsman, with the initiative usually in the bowler's hands. It is the bowler, appointed and guided by his captain, who decides whether the batsman shall have fast, medium or slow balls to deal with. He also decides the more detailed plan of attack as to how the batsman shall be tempted to make a wrong stroke. This can be effected either by easy-looking balls or by such a succession of difficult balls that the batsman mishits through sheer exasperation at not being able to score the necessary runs otherwise.

That brings us to the first basic point in bowling; what makes a ball easy or difficult to the batsman? Let us start with the latter part of the question and say that the normal first requisite of a difficult ball is that it should make the batsman feel that, if he misses it, it will hit his wicket. We will call this 'accuracy of direction'. The second point is that it should be so pitched that it arrives at an awkward angle to the bat, so that the bat may either miss it completely or, in hitting it, send it in a direction not intended by the batsman. This is referred to as 'good length'.

Now the easy ball is generally considered by batsmen to be one of three main types. It may be one which can be hit before it has pitched (full toss), one which can be hit immediately after it has pitched (half-volley), or it may be one which can be hit some time after it has pitched, after the bounce of the ball has reached its highest point (long hop). Conversely, the difficult ball is either one which the batsman can only hit exactly as it pitches, between the full toss and the half-volley (a yorker), or one which is rising from that part of the pitch between the half-volley and the long hop (a good length). The reason for these balls being difficult will be evident to anyone who has done any batting, and it has already been dealt with in greater detail in the chapter on batting. [See diagrams on pages 28 and 30.]

A glance at the above-mentioned diagrams will show

that, although the yorker may be a dangerous ball when
it is successfully bowled, it has to be pitched accurately
within an inch or two, the slightest inaccuracy turning it
into one of those balls that a batsman likes—a full pitch
or a half-volley. There is too little margin of error, so
we do not often try to bowl yorkers. On the other hand,
the good length ball can be seen to cover a greater
distance between the half-volley, to which the batsman
will play forward, and the long hop, to which he will
play back. Thus, the good length ball is the bowler's
best, partly because it does not need such accuracy as the
yorker, partly because it has to be struck as it is rising
and partly because the batsman will be in two minds
whether to play forward or to play back, and will have
the least possible amount of time in which to make up
his mind. Beyond actually mentioning it, little stress
has been laid on accuracy of direction or, in other words,
the likelihood of the ball hitting the wickets, for the
utility of this is fairly obvious; but one cannot lay too
much stress on accuracy of length, and especially the
good length, for no bowler can hope to take wickets with
any consistency unless he can control his length.

Good length balls

A good length ball on a full-sized pitch may be said
to be one that pitches about 4 yards from the batsman's wicket for a slow bowler, 5 yards for a medium-
paced bowler and 6 or 7 yards for a fast bowler. These
figures, however, can only be taken as a very rough
guide, for not only do standards differ as to what constitutes fast, medium-paced or slow bowling but also a
hard pitch will need a shorter ball than a soft pitch, as
will an individual batsman with a long reach who might
turn a normal good length ball into a half-volley. It is
evident, therefore, that a mere mechanical ability to

pitch the ball on some regular spot called a 'good length' is of little value compared with the flexible ability to pitch the ball exactly where circumstances demand that it should be pitched.

Control of length depends on two things—an easy rhythmical delivery and persistent practice. As to the former, it is generally considered best for the bowling arm (we will assume, unless specifically stated otherwise, that we are always dealing with a *right*-handed bowler) to be kept straight and to swing in an arc of a circle with the shoulder as its centre, with the arm as its radius, and with the plane of the circle at right angles to the ground; or, to put it a little less geometrically, with the arm absolutely perpendicular when the hand is at its highest point; or, to avoid geometry altogether, the ball should be delivered from the highest point that the hand can possibly reach. The more open the circle, the smoother and less jerky will be the delivery and, therefore, the greater will be the control of length. A trial of different methods will soon show that this open circle is a physical impossibility if one stands squarely facing the direction in which the ball is to go; let us call that direction 'the target'. The only way of doing it is to stand sideways, and to swing the arm up and then down across the chest. In order to bowl a ball with this swing, it will obviously be necessary to point the *left* shoulder at the target, thus improving the scope of the original circle by placing its centre at some point in the body roughly level with the lowest ribs.

The detailed study of the bowling action

A very valuable aid to the learning of any game is the ciné film, and particularly the slow-motion picture. To watch a good bowler in slow motion is far more instructive than any description in words. Such a picture of bowling—or, for that matter, of any correctly executed athletic action—will show how an impulse is started in one part of the body, usually a limb, and how it seems to ripple in a natural sequence through the various other parts of the body, all of which play their own part in directing the action along the intended lines. A boxer wishing to punch does not place his foot in one direction and then punch at right angles to it, but foot and punch follow the same direction. So it is with the bowler whom we watch by means of the slow-motion film. We see the forward impulse begin with the run-up. At the climax of this, the left starts the secondary impulse of the delivery by raising itself higher than normal, while the body is bent slightly back on the pivot of the right leg. At this stage, the whole left side of the body is pointed at the target. Then, starting with the left foot and travelling up through the body with the resilience of a whip, the circle is made, each part just a fraction of a second behind the part before it, until the ball has left the hand, and the right arm and side and leg have taken the place of those of the left, and a smooth follow-through has begun. It is only when one sees a perfectly rhythmical and poised delivery such as that of a Larwood or a Lindwall that one can appreciate the meaning of the expression 'the poetry of motion'; and it is only when a batsman is facing someone who possesses this gift that he realizes the 'nip' off the pitch and the length and directional control that it gives. Let me repeat the clue to this method—point your left shoulder at the target.

Solo Practice

As soon as the method of delivering the ball has been understood and perfected, the second way for the beginner to obtain control of length is by practice. The famous Australian Test cricketer, C. V. Grimmett, perhaps

the greatest self-made bowler of all time, is the perfect
model for this. Even after he had reached the standard
of first-class cricket, he realized the importance of constant practice, and he is reputed to have laid down a
wicket in his garden where he used to bowl and bowl and
bowl by the hour, obtaining the balls back from the stop
net at the end of each over by means of a fox-terrier
which he had specially trained for the job! The method
which is recommended for the practice of length and
direction is the simple one of a fully marked-out pitch
with a rectangle of white paint on the ground at a point
judged to be a good length for the speed of the bowler
concerned, so that a ball pitching on it will hit the
stumps.

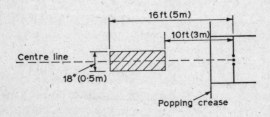

In the above diagram, a white rectangle is marked
out at an average distance of 10 to 16 feet from the
stumps, extending 18 inches in width from the line
of the leg stump towards the off side. For practice
purposes, it is a good tip to count two points for a ball
pitching in the rectangle and one point for a ball which
hits the stumps; a ball which is of correct length and
direction will thus obtain three points. If you happen
to be a left-hander or a leg-break bowler, you will have
to adjust the position of the rectangle slightly. The
method of practising is quite simple. Take your normal
run for each ball and see how many points you can score

in an over of six balls. A friend to stand beside the
rectangle acting as an 'umpire' in the case of doubtful
hits will be an advantage. Persevere until you keep on
breaking your own record of points per over.

When you feel sufficiently sure of being able to bowl
the straight good length ball whenever you wish, you
should then try to vary your length slightly, mixing an
occasional short or well-pitched-up ball in an over of
good length balls. At the same time you can practise
varying your direction by trying a series just outside the
off stump, followed by a series on or just outside the leg
stump; this is a good exercise for preparing yourself for
the sometimes unsettling left-handed batsman. It is
worth noting that bowling to a batsman in a practice
net is by no means the best kind of training for a beginner,
as the presence of a batsman is apt to confuse him at first.
Consequently, the self-teaching bowler will certainly lose
nothing by his lonely state in the early stages, a fact
which is most encouraging to the learner.

Differences of pace

Once you have mastered length and direction so that
you can pitch the ball with the minimum of error just
where you wish, the next quality common to all good
bowlers is variety of pace. This sounds easy enough on
the face of it, but change of pace does not mean the
ability in a fast bowler to produce an occasional 'dolly-
drop' that soars into the sky and drops in a lifeless way
half-way up the pitch, so that the batsman, after he has
recovered from his surprise, has ample time to charge
up the pitch to it and strike it hard in any direction he
chooses. Nor does it mean the ability of a slow bowler
suddenly to galvanize himself into a hurricane of whirl-
ing arms and legs, which culminate in a thunderbolt of a
long hop or a full toss which the batsman also welcomes

as being a pleasant change from the cunning breaks that the slow bowler had previously been sending down. Even if the length is good, such extreme variations are not very effective—and they certainly tend to demoralize the unfortunate wicket-keeper! No, variation of pace is something much more subtle than that.

To start with, the change of pace must not be apparent to the batsman until he is actually playing the ball. In other words, he should be encouraged to make exactly the same stroke as he made to the previous ball, and if there is too obvious a change in pace he will not do so. So what is needed is a very *slight* change of pace with no alteration of action; in fact, there should be just the merest holding back of the delivery swing or loosening of the wrist for the slower ball and the use of just a tiny bit more body in the delivery swing or a tightening of the wrist for the faster ball.

Finger spin

The last of the technical skills that the aspiring bowler should try to master are those of spin—or break—and swerve—or swing. It is very seldom that a bowler will be found who is skilful in all the different kinds of spin and swerve, but every bowler finds that a selection of two or three of them is useful. Let us take spin first. A ball after pitching may change direction from the leg (a leg-break), or from the off (an off-break), or it may make haste off the pitch (a top-spinner). Broadly speaking, there are two ways of producing these breaks. One is by means of the fingers, clicking them as we sometimes do in order to attract the attention of a dog; this is known as 'finger spin'. The other way is by changing the position of the hand as the ball leaves it, thus rolling the ball out and making it spin in a certain direction; this is called 'rolled spin'. On the whole, finger spin is used by slow bowlers and rolled spin by medium-paced and fast bowlers. In both cases, the ball must leave either by the front of the hand, emerging between the thumb and first finger, for the off-break, or by the back of the hand, emerging outside the little finger, for the leg-break.

The way in which a bowler grips the ball is particularly important for spin. First and foremost, a bowler does not hold the ball in his hand. It is all fingers, and the principle is to get as much friction between the fingers and the ball as possible, so as to start it spinning at the same time as it is being propelled forward. In this respect, there are two main schools of thought. Some like to hold the ball so that the seam, the one rough part of the ball, lies parallel with and between the first and middle fingers, with the thumb touching it round the other side. This method is probably better for the off-break than for the leg-break. [*See* Figures (*a*) and (*b*) on pages 84 and 85.] Others like to use as many fingers as possible, and the only way to do this is to have the seam running at right angles to the fingers. [*See* Figures (*c*) and (*d*) on pages 87 and 88.] An adaptation of this grip was the one used by Sidney Barnes, perhaps the greatest medium-paced spin bowler of all time; his great asset was that the batsmen could not tell which kind of break he was bowling until the ball whipped off the pitch from leg or off. He held the ball with the second and third fingers across the seam, with the *inside* of the forefinger and little finger lying along the seam, and it only needed a last-second flick with one or other of these and a stroke with the top of the thumb to turn the ball into either a leg- or an off-break. [*See* Figure (*e*) on page 89.]

A bowler—and also a captain—should know what conditions of pitch and ball will help spin bowling and which will hamper it. Generally speaking, a spin bowler prefers a ball that has lost its shine; at any rate, shine is

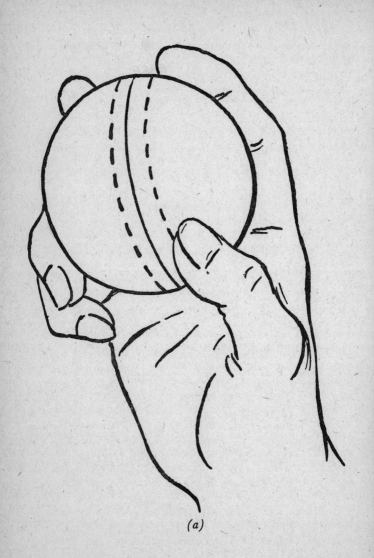

(a)

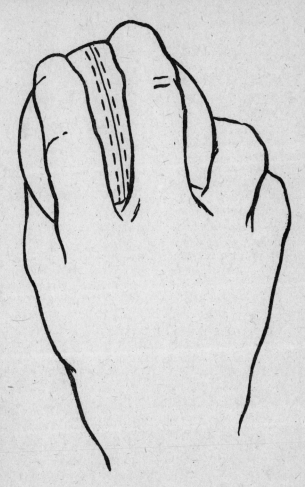

(b)

not necessary for spin. The ball must also be dry, but for the matter of that, no bowler likes to bowl with a wet, slippery ball; for then his control of length and direction becomes a more chancy matter. For spin to be effective the pitch has to be of a consistency that allows the ball to bite when it pitches. Very dry, hard wickets of the consistency of baked clay give the ball little to bite on; and a very soft, wet wicket, while taking the spin, slows the ball up so much that the batsman has plenty of time to see it.

The type of pitch that helps a spin bowler most is one that *has* been wet and soft but that is in the process of drying. There is a slight sponginess underneath a thin surface of hardess; the surface gives speed off the pitch and the sponginess below helps the spin to bite. Spin bowlers have many a time been seen rubbing their hands with glee during an evening thunderstorm, in anticipation of the glut of wickets they expect on the morrow, when the sun is drying the wicket and doing its best to make their spin unplayable.

Making the ball swerve

Swerve is the movement of a ball when it changes direction in mid-air. The ball, after leaving the bowler's hand, may swing either from the off or from the leg, generally known as in-swing and out-swing respectively, and this swing is obtained by gripping the ball correctly, coupled with some inherent ability in the action of the particular bowler. Figure (*b*) on page 85 is generally considered to be the best type of grip for swerve bowling and the ball should slide out from between the ends of the first and second fingers. The off-swerve is imparted by swinging the arm up over the head and down away from the body, while the leg-swerve is imparted by a slightly round arm swing where the arm at its highest point is not quite vertical; in each case it is helpful for the body to follow the arm.

Advantageous conditions for swerve bowling are:

1. A new ball, or at least a shiny ball; it is the shiny and polished surface of the ball which makes it side-slip through the air. It is therefore often easy to spot a swing bowler from a distance by the way in which, as he walks back for his run, he rubs the ball on his trousers or shirt in order to give it this necessary polish.

2. The atmosphere; this is a most important factor in swerve bowling. It is generally better for a swing bowler

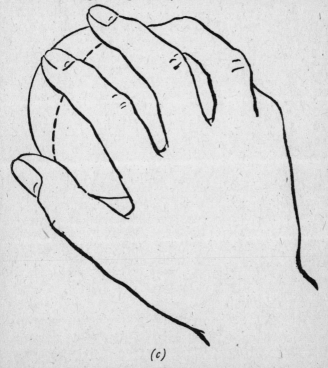

(c)

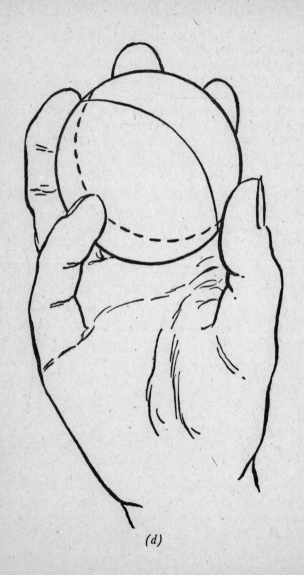

(d)

to bowl either into the wind or with the wind coming
from the side where he needs most help for his swerve;
but the density of the atmosphere itself has a great deal
to do with swerve, even without any wind at all. This
density varies from day to day and from ground to ground,
and on low-lying grounds in heavy, sultry weather it
frequently happens that swing bowlers have the utmost
difficulty in keeping the ball on the wicket, so strong has
been the swerve caused by the atmosphere. On the other
hand, there are often occasions when the most pro-

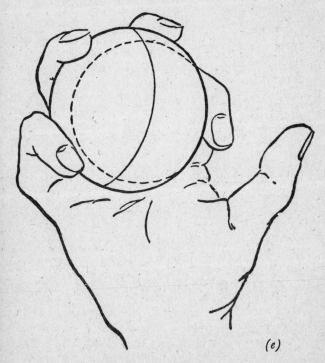

(e)

THE BARNES GRIP

nounced of swing bowlers, even with a new ball, have been hard put to it to make the ball move an inch out of the straight.

Fast bowling

So far we have spoken of bowling in general terms only. It is now time to particularize and to give some hints on how to become either a fast, medium-paced or slow bowler. To a fast bowler, all that has been said about the easy rhythmical delivery is of the first importance, for a fast bowler's worst enemy is fatigue, and one does not want to develop a tiring, unrhythmical action which is only effective for three or four overs. Let us take things in order and start with the run up to the wicket. A fast bowler must make his run exact and automatic. It must be exact because he has to plant his right foot as near to the target as the rules allow without giving a 'no ball', in order to have the greatest amount of control over his length and to make the trajectory of the ball as steep as possible. It must be automatic because he has no time to watch where his right foot should be planted at the moment of delivery. The next point is the question of how to hold the ball, and fast bowlers on the whole agree that the grip shown in Figures (a) and (b) on pages 84 and 85 is the best for their purpose. Lastly, in order to avoid any possible checking of pace, a strong follow-through of three or four paces is generally considered necessary.

A fast bowler's usual methods of getting a batsman out are as follows:

1. Hitting the wicket. This is usually done by an off-break, by a yorker or by sheer speed. In order not to bounce over the wicket, however, the ball has to be well pitched up and can often be played as a half-volley, which you

will remember, is one of the batsman's 'easy balls'. So, while keeping the batsman always worrying about the safety of his wicket, our fast bowler must often be prepared to try some other method of getting him out.

2. Making the batsman touch the ball into the hands of the wicket-keeper, slips or gully. The kind of ball which is most likely to do this is an out-swinger, pitching on or near the off stump so as to make the batsman reach out to play it and then swinging away towards the off. The batsman thinks the ball is coming close to him, but owing to the swing from the leg it just avoids the middle of his bat and, finding its edge instead, is deflected into the waiting hands of the fielders behind the wicket.

3. By bowling 'leg theory'. This means bowling at the leg stump and pitching an occasional ball rather short of the length, with some extra lift and fire off the pitch imparted by increasing pace and a whip-lash delivery. A bumper can then be produced which often makes a physically nervous batsman play a blind defensive stroke, thus sending an easy catch either to mid-off, the bowler himself, mid-on or short-leg. This kind of bowling is generally considered to be bad and unsportsmanlike cricket if indulged in too frequently and persistently by fast bowlers; but there can be no harm in occasionally reminding the batsman that he *may* be struck by the ball! That is one of the risks which make cricket a man's game; otherwise we would play with a soft ball!

The 'field' on page 92 allows for one spare man, who can be placed at any one of the five positions marked by panels: extra-cover, silly mid-off, short fine-leg, deep fine-leg or deep square-leg. A really fast bowler might prefer this extra man at third slip, alongside the other two, but to afford this luxury the conditions must be ideal for slip catches. The final choice is a matter for the bowler and his captain, and will depend on the batsman, the situation of the game and the directional accuracy of the bowler.

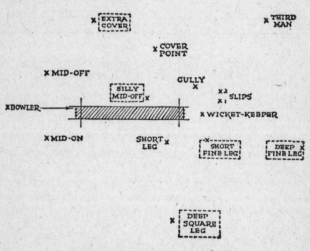

A PLAN FOR A FAST BOWLER'S FIELD

Medium-paced bowling

Medium-paced bowlers are the patient hard-workers of a team. Their bowling is not as energetic as that of the fast bowler, but for that reason they are expected to continue for much longer periods at a stretch. Also, since their speed through the air is so much slower, it is much easier for the batsman to see the ball; consequently, they have to rely on cunning combined with spin and swerve in order to outwit the batsman and make him play that false stroke, which may prove his undoing in any of the five ways mentioned at the start of this chapter. Yet it is vital for the medium-paced bowler to realize that swing and spin and cunning are useless without the Three Controls—control of length, control of direction and control of flight (or change of pace). It is often the case that a steady length for over after over, with the ball pitching regularly just short of the half-volley, will tantalize the batsman into attempting a wild unsuitable scoring stroke which will get him out. So when a medium-paced bowler hears one of his victims cursing his own impetuosity and saying that he got himself out to a perfectly easy ball, he may quietly pat himself on the back and hope that all his other opponents may be so lulled into that false sense of security which thinks there is no harm in that steady, apparently guileless, but good length bowling of his.

There are, however, more interesting ways in which a medium-paced bowler may dismiss the batsman, some or all of which may be tried concurrently without even the most experienced and intelligent of bowlers being able to predict which method will actually take the wicket. Here are a few of the most frequently successful methods for our medium-paced bowler to consider:

1. He may vary his length for three or four balls of an over, maybe allowing the batsman to score, but leaving him in no doubt as to whether he should play back or forward; then he sends down a couple on the good length spot which catch his opponent in two minds as to which he should do. The result, if the length is right, will be an inconclusive shot, neither one thing nor the other, with a consequent mishitting of the ball, even if it is not missed completely. In this respect, the great advantage to any bowler slower than fast-medium is that a good length

ball will not normally bounce over the stumps if it is missed by the batsman but should, under average conditions, neatly flick off the bails.

2. Another method is to bowl three or four balls on or just outside the off stump, moving away from the leg. Whichever way the batsman plays these, you may presume that he will expect another of the same type; but instead of that you give him, disguised as best you can, one that pitches on the same spot but that either goes straight through or breaks or swings in from the off. This takes him by surprise and causes him to play outside the ball, so that it passes between his bat and his body to hit the stumps, or even strikes his body and causes him to be out l.b.w. A batsman returning to the pavilion may often be heard condemning his bad luck and saying 'It pitched well outside the off stump, but I played it on'. Nine times out of ten that is not bad luck at all, but just a good piece of bowling.

3. It will be seen from these two examples that a medium-paced bowler must depend very largely on a progressive scheme for his wickets; and various modifications of the above can be worked out so as to use to the best advantage the bowler's special abilities, combined often with some unobtrusively given instructions to certain key fieldsmen. There is, for instance, the scheme whereby at the start of an over you quietly motion extra cover to a deeper position. You then begin the over with a well-pitched-up ball, perhaps even a half-volley, just outside the off stump; this is followed with one the same length but a few inches wider; the next a few inches wider than that, and so on. The hope is that the batsman will not notice how each delivery is gradually veering to the off and that, sooner or later, he will fail to get his left foot quite to the pitch of the ball and thus send a catch to cover or extra cover. Such progressive schemes, unfortunately, are sometimes shaken by the particular batsman on whom you are concentrating obtaining a single or a three and leaving for the other end. For that reason, it sometimes suits a bowler deliberately to miss a return throw to his wicket in order that an extra run may be made on the overthrow and the desired batsman return to face the bowling.

The medium-paced bowler who has the ability to spin the ball or make it swerve should be wary of over-using all the kinds of ball he can bowl. He should remember that it is the unexpected that really gets the wickets, and so he must decide on some stock ball, which may vary according to the day or the individual batsman, and then peg away with it, only producing something different when he feels the batsman is not expecting it. The average medium-paced bowler will find that a leg-break is not easy to bowl accurately; in fact, many very successful ones, such as Maurice Tate, hardly employed it at all, being content to use swing only in order to move the ball from the leg, with both swing and break to move it from the off. Remember that the off-break is the natural one for right-arm bowlers, many of whom find it quite hard *not* to bowl with an off-break, The stock ball, then, will usually be the off-break, with the leg-swinger, the straight one or the off-swinger as occasional surprises. The stock target may be the off stump or just outside it, with an occasional stab at the leg stump. The stock length will be the good length, with an occasional yorker or even high full toss. Finally, the stock pace will be a steady medium, with the occasional quicker or slower one slipped in with the minimum amount of advertisement.

As can be seen from the diagram on page 96, the eleventh fielder can be placed at second slip—this is advisable for fast-medium bowling—at mid-wicket or on the boundary behind the bowler, at long-on or long-off.

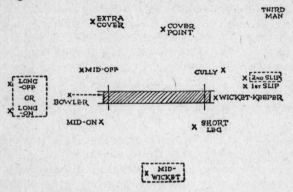

THE NORMAL MEDIUM-PACED BOWLER'S FIELD

Slow bowling

The slow bowler, like the medium-paced, very often has to be patient and long-suffering, although on a sticky or crumbling pitch he may experience such resounding success as the medium-paced bowler seldom enjoys. Psychologically, he has to be imperturbable; he must not lose his head if the batsmen hit sixes off him and he must not get a swelled head or over-confident if he manages to take some quick wickets. Like bowlers of other speeds he depends for success on a perfect command of length, which can only be obtained by constant practice, but his main armament is the leg-break coupled with flight. The off-break is useful as a variation, and so is the ball which goes straight through without any break at all; but these are of little use as attacking balls by themselves.

Let us take the slow bowler's length first. It should be his aim to bowl so as to encourage the batsman to play forward, either defensively or offensively, even to the extent of over-pitching and bowling half-volleys. It is easy to tell if you are pitching them short of a length by the fact that the batsman will be comfortably playing back to them. This is often a most deceptive state of affairs to an inexperienced bowler, who is apt to think that he is therefore 'on top' of the batsman, whereas what is really happening is that he is giving the batsman some free batting practice just to get his eye in; and after an over or two he will probably begin to show how he has benefited from that practice!

A slow bowler may often find himself bowling on a pitch that will not take spin, or he may find himself bowling to a batsman who is set and who is seeing the ball so well that he is confidently and successfully taking all the risks which the bowler hoped he would take hesitatingly. Under such circumstances, probably the only way of taking a wicket is by keeping to a perfect, unvarying length, dropping the ball steadily on the same square foot of turf for over after over. The word 'dropping' is used advisedly, for it must be remembered that a ball from any but fast and fast-medium bowlers must leave the bowler's hand in an upward direction and follow a more or less curving line down to the ground at the other end of the pitch. In fact, it is this 'dropping' pitch of the ball on the ground which enables the slow bowler to spin the ball more than the faster bowlers. Arriving at a more vertical angle, it has a better chance of biting on the turf and turning off at a sharp angle.

That slow bowler's curve through the air aids not only spin but also flight. If the ball goes a few inches higher than usual after it has left the bowler's hand, it will take a fraction of a second longer to complete the curve (always supposing that the length is the same) and will therefore reach the batsman a fraction of a second later than he is expecting it. The result is that he will

T.Y.C.—5

play too soon, the bat either crossing the line of the flight before the ball arrives or reaching the ball when it is beginning to follow through in an upward direction, thereby cocking the ball up in the air. This late arrival of the ball—or conversely, its early arrival where the curve is less than usual, thus making the batsman play late instead of early—must not be advertised by any change of action. It must be the same smooth concentration of forces that was described at the beginning of the chapter and that was stressed for the fast bowler; but the slower ball can be produced by letting go a little sooner and relaxing the wrist, and the faster one by letting go later with a stiffened wrist. If there is no hint of change in the delivery, the batsman will hardly know what to expect until the ball arrives, for the higher or lower trajectory of the ball is almost impossible to gauge unless the change is exaggerated. The faster ball as well as the slower ball has been mentioned, but the latter is actually far more dangerous to the batsman, and it is for this reason that slow bowlers generally like to bowl *into* any wind that is blowing, for a sudden gust may slow up the ball even though the bowler himself is unaware of the fact.

Let us now return to the question of spin, the slow bowler's main armament. Before we go any further, it is necessary that we should divide our slow bowlers into right-arm and left-arm and treat them separately, for where spin is so vitally concerned the policy of the left-hander will vary considerably from that of the right-hander. It has already been said that the leg-break is the slow bowler's most dangerous ball, but to the right-arm bowler it is very difficult to bowl because it is so unnatural. Whatever grip is employed, it is bowled by turning the wrist with the back of the hand to the batsman, so as to deliver the ball from the little finger side of the hand, with the arm going over considerably quicker than the ball is to travel through the air. By turning the wrist a little more, a top-spinner is bowled; this will go straight through after pitching. By turning the wrist still more, that nightmare of the unwatchful batsman—the 'googly'—is produced, a ball that is bowled with a leg-break action but that breaks from the off instead.

The leg-break, googly and top-spinner are difficult to tell apart, and they are, therefore, the best possible combination for the slow bowler, so long as he remembers that variety is the best way of keeping the batsman guessing. It is worth while, then, to practise these three spinners together. 'Practise them together' is an important rule, because if they are practised separately for any length of time a bowler is liable to lose the knack of one or other, and they are most valuable when all three are bowled equally well. It is important, too, to keep them going all the time; so, when normal practice conditions are impossible, try them indoors, under-arm with a tennis ball if necessary.

It is not as easy to pick out three or four stock ways of taking wickets for the slow bowler as it was for the medium and fast bowlers. Wickets often come to the slow bowler in surprising ways, often not planned for in any detail, but a glance at the diagram of the slow right-hander's field will give some idea of what can be done. Two main principles can, however, be put forward. First of all, the batsman must be encouraged to hit hard; so often in all classes of the game, from village to test cricket, reports read that a particular batsman 'hit a six to deep square-leg but was then caught on the boundary off the very next ball in an attempt to repeat the stroke'. The second principle is to make the batsman hit against the break, for it is much easier to hit a slow ball with the break than against it. There are various ways of encouraging a sluggish batsman to hit out; one of these is to place the field so as to leave an obvious gap which he will try to reach; another is to pitch the ball well up to him; and a further one as a last resort is to bowl an occasionally easy long hop or a guileless looking full toss. It largely depends on your summing-up of the batsman's temperament. In order to force the batsman to hit against the break, it is best to bowl off-breaks outside the off-stump breaking on to the wicket or, better still, leg-breaks on the leg stump also breaking on to the wicket.

There are two main ways in which the googly or top-spin bowler takes his wickets. The only difference between them is in the direction of the stock ball, which is a leg-break. In the first method it may be bowled on the leg stump, which tends to pin the batsman down if the length is good, for he dare not hit against the break and he will lay bare his wicket if he steps outside it to play it with the break towards the off side. By way of variety, the bowler sends down a googly or top-spinner on the off stump, and the batsman, expecting another leg-break, thinks he sees his chance to hit with the break; but, because of the unexpected spin, he plays outside it. In the other method, the stock leg-break pitches on the off stump, and, whether the batsman gets control over it or not, it is equally disconcerting for him when he finds what looks like an exactly similar ball going straight through or else turning from the off. The result is often a case of l.b.w. It should be added that the top-spinner, though not so sensational, is very nearly as useful as the googly. The reason for this has already been given—a little variation is all that is required to evade or find the edge of a bat 4 inches wide.

A slow right-arm bowler's field

Depending on the favourite scoring strokes of the individual batsman, the 'field' on page 101 allows for the eleventh fielder to be placed at deep extra-cover or silly mid-off or deep mid-wicket.

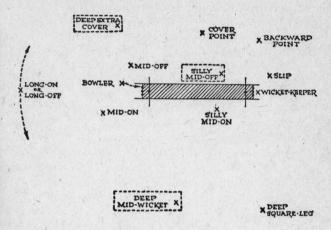

Slow left-arm bowling

It will be seen from the diagram of the slow right-arm bowler's field that the fielders are placed in the deep in three different directions. This really demonstrates his weakness. It is necessary to have the boundary in front of the wicket well guarded, because the leg-break, googly and top-spinner are all awkward balls to bowl, and are therefore difficult to deliver accurately. How lucky, then, is the left-hander to find that the leg-break, which is so important as the slow bowler's stock ball, comes naturally to him and can therefore be easily bowled with accurate length and direction. The stock ball, owing to this greater accuracy, becomes a wicket-taker in itself. So the first principle for a left-hander should be to bowl in such a way that the batsman can only hit the ball into an off-side field. This involves pitching the ball well up, on or near the off stump, with the occasional

ball that comes straight through with the left arm—
equivalent to the right-arm top-spinner—and the very
occasional one which pitches outside the off stump and
then breaks in from the off. This last named type is
known as the 'chinaman' and bowlers have considerable
difficulty in bowling it accurately. We have the example
of a famous line of past left-arm slow bowlers—men like
Wilfred Rhodes, J. C. White and Hedley Verity—to
prove the worth of that relentless hammering at the
same spot, which forces the batsman to play continually
into the crowded covers, while at the same time he
is constantly aware of the wide open spaces on the
leg side towards which it would be fatal to play the
ball.

A further advantage which the slow left-hander enjoys
over the slow right-hander is best illustrated by the
diagram below.

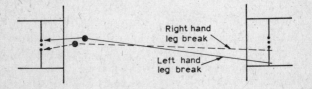

This diagram has been deliberately fore-shortened so
as to illustrate the impression which the batsman has
while the ball is in the air before it pitches on a line
between the stumps. From the right-handed bowler,
the ball appears to be going to hit the leg stump if it
does not break, but from the left-hander it seems to be
curling away for an easy shot to leg if it does not break.
In other words, the left-hander's delivery from 3 or 4
feet wide of the stumps often gives the batsman a false
sense of confidence, especially if he is fond of leg-side
play.

Here is a typical *slow left-arm bowler's field*:

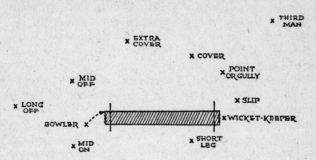

Some useful tips

A bowler's job is to try to deceive the batsman, and in order to do that he must discover what the batsman is expecting, what he is thinking and what he is feeling. Lacking any direct information on the subject, he must study the batsman from the moment he arrives in sight from the pavilion, rather as a psychoanalyst studies a patient! The stance of a batsman will often give a hint of the kind of stroke he hopes to be able to play. If he leans on his front foot he is probably keen on playing back whenever possible, whereas if he puts his weight on his back foot he is probably a forward player by choice. Watch carefully to see whether he is an offensive batsman on the look-out for runs or whether he is a stick-in-the-mud who needs to be encouraged to take risks. See whether he favours off-side or on-side play and whether he is quick on his feet or rather firm footed. Then when you think you have learnt his particular likes and dislikes, it is sometimes the better policy to feed his favourite stroke (having first placed a suitable field) rather than his bad stroke, for it is often the fact that the batsman is aware of his weakness and therefore plays the difficult stroke with more care than the easy one.

The general system of placing a field should be that of two rings round the batsman, an inner and an outer ring, the former to make him hit hard and the latter to deal with the results of that hitting. With a new batsman it is always worth while to place one or two fieldsmen close in to snap up any ball that he may play awkwardly in the opening stages of hs innings.

The moving of a fieldsman is an important point. Call him by a sharp clap of the hands and make sure that he goes exactly to the spot where you want him. It is sometimes a good trick to place a man somewhere, at square-leg say, with a pre-arranged sign to move deeper a yard or two each ball, and then when he is just where you want him you bowl the long hop which you are sure the batsman has been pining for.

All bowlers, but particularly slow bowlers, should be ready to field their own bowling, for an opportunity for 'caught and bowled' comes very often, but it is frequently wasted by the bowler being taken by surprise at the sudden return of the ball towards himself. A really keen and active bowler can, in fact, almost field as his own short mid-off by following up quickly after he has delivered the ball. When the batsman takes a run, especially if it is a quick one, the bowler should immediately place himself behind the stumps, with the stumps between himself and the place where the ball has gone. Then, if the fieldsman throws down the wicket, the bowler will not be in the way of the ball, while if the throw misses the wicket, he can gather it for a possible run out. Yet a word of warning to the bowler is necessary in either of these two cases; it is not cowardly behaviour but common sense to avoid stopping a hard return with your bowling hand when there is no chance of a run-out decision. If that hand is damaged, the side loses a bowler—a serious loss to any captain.

After rain, it is often necessary for a bowler to bowl

with a wet ball. Many bowlers are content to use sawdust in order to dry off that slippery dampness, but the best way is to provide the umpire with an old piece of towel or dish cloth so that you can dry the ball on it when it becomes difficult to control. Sawdust, however, is often vitally necessary to prevent the bowler's foot from slipping as he releases the ball, and it should be scattered liberally around the bowling crease, especially for a fast bowler, whose accuracy depends largely on a firm foothold. One final tip—*a boy of fourteen or under should always bowl with a small-sized ball ($4\frac{3}{4}$ oz) on a pitch of 20 yards or less*. He will learn nothing of spin, swerve or length if he tries to practise these under conditions which are suitable only for grown men.

CHAPTER 6

Fielding

A considerable amount about the art of fielding has already been written in the chapters concerned primarily with batting and bowling, but fielding is such an important branch of cricket that it deserves at least a short chapter to itself. Assuming that the reader is literally keen enough to follow the title of this book and to try to teach himself cricket, the probability is that he really enjoys fielding already. To every cricketer except the slow thinker and the ponderous runner, fielding is—or should be—jolly good fun. There is a delight and pride in chasing a ball which is speeding towards the boundary, cutting it off with a one-handed pick up and immediately hurling it in to the wicket-keeper's hands 6 inches above the bails. Such an action is, of course, the hallmark of the accomplished fieldsman, but keeness plays a bigger part in this branch of the game than it does in any other. Batting and bowling demand a considerable amount of skill and adaptation to certain recognized rules and standards; fielding's main requisite is enthusiasm. As a result, many boys who cannot bat or bowl thoroughly enjoy the fun of fielding. First of all, let us study the diagram on page 107 which gives the names of the many positions which a fielder can take up during play.

Of course, only eleven of the above positions can be filled at any one time and even they are not absolutely fixed points. For instance, square-leg can be placed near the umpire or very deep right out on the boundary; point can move to backward-point and so save a gully;

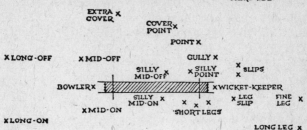

mid-off and mid-on can be deep or close in according to circumstances, and so on. Certain positions require certain natural attributes; thus out-fielders like long-on, deep mid-wicket, third man, extra-cover and long-leg should be primarily fast runners and good judges of high catches, whereas in-fielders like short-leg, silly point and the slips require quick reaction without much leg movement. As these individual attributes will be considered later, let us first deal with generalizations.

The first stage in teaching yourself to become a good fielder is to anticipate where the ball is going by carefully watching the bat. Every member of the side should be 'on his toes' as the bowler runs up to deliver the ball, and, except in the case of those fielding close to the batsman, they should walk in a few paces towards the wicket in anticipation of the ball being hit in their direction. Usually it is best to make sure of stopping the ball by keeping the feet close together behind the hands, but this method, although safe, lessens the chances of obtaining a run out, the joy and ambition of every

fielder. So, whenever there is a possibility of taking a
wicket, a certain amount of risk may be taken and the
fieldsman continues his walk towards the striker, even
breaking into a run in order to meet the ball rather than
waiting for it; this involves a one-handed pick up, so the
eyes must be kept glued to the moving ball.

Throwing-in

The next stage is the throw. On the vast majority of
occasions, the ball should be returned to the wicket-
keeper, who, unlike the bowler, is gloved and padded
and in position next to the stumps. The ideal return is a
full pitch straight into the wicket-keeper's hands a few
inches above the bails, and all players fielding within
30 yards of the batsman should make this their objective.
The actual throw can be below or above the shoulder,
but the former is harder to control, especially as regards
direction. For those fielding at a considerable distance
from the striker, the aim should be to throw it to the
wicket-keeper in such a way that the ball arrives in his
hands on the long hop; half-volleys and returns along the
ground only make things difficult for him. If there is a
real chance of a run out, the ball can be returned
quickly to the bowler's end, but remember that his hands
are valuable assets to the side, and he should not be
expected to risk an injury to them by stopping a lightning
full toss or an unpleasantly bouncing return near the
ground.

Catching

Catching is another branch of fielding, and it is almost
entirely a matter of practice. If you are a beginner,
practise taking all kinds of catches—snicks, slow high
ones, gentle low ones and high drives. Later on, you can

do a certain amount of specializing by becoming primarily a slip fielder or a deep field; but no cricketer
should ever develop into such a specialist that he cannot
take his place in any position on the field, unless it be
that of wicket-keeper. Catching in the slips is no easy
matter; the ball comes off the edge of the bat so swiftly
that the fieldsman has to be extraordinarily quick, so
quick, in fact, that he should hold his hands in front
of him in readiness, as he will have little time for movement. Gully must be even quicker in his reactions;
but, generally speaking, the further away from the bat a
fieldsman stands, the more time he has to collect his
thoughts, to get well underneath the ball as it drops, to
make a neat cup with his hands and to 'give' slightly
as the ball enters that cup. A slip-catching machine is
very helpful; failing that, skidding the ball off the top
of a roller is an excellent game for two or three boys on
each side of the roller.

A combined catching and throwing practice can be
carried out for a few minutes each day by a number of
enthusiasts. One acts as a batsman, and he takes three
or four balls out on to the field and stands about 10
yards to the side of a stump, behind which is a wicket-
keeper. The batsman hits each ball in turn into the
air, at the same time calling out the name of the fieldsman he wishes to catch it. As each fielder collects a
ball, he throws it full toss or on the long hop to the top
of the stump, where the wicket-keeper practises running
out an imaginary opponent.

Qualifications for fielding positions

While it is not a good thing, especially for a beginner,
to specialize too seriously on one or two positions in the
field, each member of a cricket team is likely to possess
certain physical attributes which will automatically fit

him for some positions better than others. Very briefly,
here are a few of the main qualifications which will be
advantageous for some of the most important places, ex-
cluding the wicket-keeper, who is so much of a specialist
that a special chapter (7) has been allotted him:

1. *Cover-point*

This is one of the key positions on the field, because with
a steady bowler keeping the ball on or outside the off
stump, a very large percentage of the batsmen's strokes
will send the ball in his direction. Cover-point should
take up his position 20 to 35 yards from the bat according to the class of cricket, and he should be the type of
fieldsman who can pounce swiftly on the ball, pick it up
with either hand and return it smartly to the wicket-
keeper. If you happen to possess an ambidextrous player
on your side, cover is probably the place for him, as he
will save valuable time if he has not to transfer the ball
from one hand to the other before his return to the
keeper. Cover must also be a brilliant catch, as drives
which have been slightly mistimed will hurtle through
the air at him to left or right, high or low. Like many off-
side fielders, he must remember that a driven ball will
tend to swing towards or away from his left hand, and
many of his catches will be spinning vigorously.

2. *Third man*

Speed round the boundary edge, ability to pick up on
the run and accurate long-distance throwing are the
main requisites for third man. Catches are comparat-
ively rare in this position, but, as third man often goes
to long field at the end of the over, it is a mistake to
imagine that he need not be a good catcher, for it is
obviously impossible for any player to field at third
man at both ends! As a general principle, his chief
task is to 'save the two'; a cut or sliced drive in his

direction will usually be a certain run, and it will become two runs if he hesitates before returning the ball to the wicket-keeper. Mentally, it is an easy position, because there is no need for great concentration on every ball.

3. *Mid-off*

This is an important position in every class of cricket, because it is such a good place for a captain to field. From mid-off, the captain can so easily advise and encourage the bowler. His exact position will vary slightly according to the batsman and the bowler; thus for a defensive batsman, mid-off can move up to within about 18 yards of the bat, but for a strong attacking batsman he is usually 25 to 30 yards away. His main job is to stop and hold all the off-drives within his reach. Many balls which are well pitched up and in the vicinity of the off stump will be hit hard and firmly along the ground in mid-off's direction. If these are mistimed slightly, a possible catch will often result, but it is likely to be a hard catch, hard in the sense that the ball will be travelling fast rather than one requiring acrobatic ability to reach and hold it. Consequently many mid-offs are solidly built fellows with large tough hands! Yet they cannot afford to be stolid and inactive because they must be ready to dash in to counter the semi-defensive push stroke which sends the ball slowly in their direction and gives the batsman a quick run if mid-off is a slow starter.

4. *Mid-on*

One of the few places on the cricket field where it is possible to 'hide' a poor fielder is mid-on. Like his counter-part, mid-off, the exact position he occupies will vary according to circumstances; but, unlike mid-off, he will have far fewer drives to stop or catches to hold. The reason is simply that it is easier for a batsman to drive a ball on the off side, the bad balls outside the leg stump being generally placed more squarely in the direction of the umpire or mid-wicket.

5. *Slip fielders*

According to the type of bowler and the condition of the pitch, there may be one, two, three or even, very occasionally, four slips. Comparative immobility of foot, extraordinary quickness of eye, arms, hands and fingers, and intense concentration are the main attributes of a first-class slip fielder. Literally every ball must be watched with extreme care, and it is a great mental strain to field for a long time at slip, concentrating as each ball is delivered and relaxing immediately after-wards. One hot summer afternoon at Bristol, W. R. Hammond stood for nearly four hours at slip without a ball going anywhere near him, and then, suddenly, a waist-high snick flashed off the bat, out shot Hammond's right hand and the catch was held. So a good slip fielder watches every ball in the hope that a snick will come his way, and although he will naturally be disappointed time after time when the occasion does come he must be ready to seize his opportunity.

6. *Long-off and Long-on*

It has already been stated that third man often fields in the deep for alternate overs, so his ability to run, pick up and throw will come in very useful. But, whereas third man does not often have the chance of making catches, long-off and long-on must be able to judge high catches perfectly. A slow bowler especially depends on the deep fielders to accept all the chances given them, particularly when he has persevered for a long time to persuade a batsman to risk a high drive. Judging distance so as to be right under the ball as it falls is therefore a key qualifica-tion for a deep field; and in that connection, he must resist the natural tendency to run in immediately to meet any high ball which is hit in his direction.

Those, then are the main differences between some of the common-to-all positions on the cricket field. Yet by far the best method of teaching yourself fielding is not by theory but by practice. Try to field for some time in as many different positions as possible before you make up your mind as to which particular place you prefer and then go and watch an expert. Wherever your captain tells you to stand, see that you remain there; nothing is more irritating to a captain or a bowler than to find his fielders constantly wandering from the positions in which he placed them. Above all, show keenness and enthusiasm; the amount of fun and enjoyment you will obtain from fielding is proportional to the amount of eagerness and zest you put into it.

CHAPTER 7

Wicket-keeping

Once a side takes the field, the wicket-keeper is the most important member. For that reason, when an eleven is chosen, the best wicket-keeper should be selected, quite irrespective of his batting. In what is rather loosely called junior cricket, the standard of wicket-keeping is generally well below that of the other departments of the game. It is curious that so few boys seem keen on wicket-keeping when they take up cricket; the probable reason is that some additional equipment is required in the way of special pads and gloves. This chapter will therefore be divided into two main sections. The first section makes some suggestions which, it is hoped, will encourage some keen fielders to take up wicket-keeping and then gives them some general advice. The second section is for those who have already found an interest in keeping wicket, and they can well omit the first section.

It should be emphasized at this stage that it is often of great value for a team to have a spare wicket-keeper, who is not just a fielder with gloves and pads on. In all classes of cricket, from school to test matches, the proper wicket-keeper is sometimes injured and the side usually suffers from a poor substitute. To bat in front of a first-class 'keeper', who will never allow you to lift your back foot for a fraction of a second and then, later, in front of an indifferent performer, who stands back for medium-paced bowling and allows you to advance that valuable foot or two out of your crease, will make you realize the importance of what is called an aggressive wicket-keeper. His job is to co-operate with the bowlers and never allow the batsman to settle down and feel really comfortable at the wicket.

How to start as a wicket-keeper

Few boys without previous experience will like to volunteer to keep wicket in a game, so when your friends are practising bowling to one another borrow a pair of comfortable gloves of the right size and stand behind the stumps. Put on pads, too, if you like; but the gloves are the essential part. Your first intention should be to stop every ball bowled; the feeling that when you miss the ball you must run after it will help you in that determination. At the same time see how many times you can stump the batsman. There is one guiding principle in connection with the use of your hands and it is this— keep them together, with the fingers pointing *downwards*. Try to get used to ignoring the movements of the batsman and his bat, and assume that he is going to miss every ball. Only then will you fail to be caught napping when he does miss one. It is not really a good idea to practise in the nets, although it may be better than nothing. The objection is that, when you have a net behind you, you will not bother to stop balls which you do not like, with the result that you fall into the disastrous frame of mind of a wicket-keeper who is allowed a fielder at long stop.

Elementary principles

Once you have made a start in this way, try keeping wicket in an actual game. Make sure that you have the proper equipment—a pair of under-gloves, a body protector, proper pads, and some footwear more solid and resistant than gym shoes. There is nothing more painful

than a fast full pitch landing on your toe! For all slow
bowling, stand right up to the wicket, slightly on the off
side. For medium and fast bowling, stand back at least
3 yards so that the ball of good length comes comfortably into your hands. For all balls except those on
the leg side, keep the left foot absolutely firm and only
move the right foot for balls well on the off. For a ball
that is going to be on the leg side, move *both* your feet
across so that you stand with your body just beyond that
of the batsman. Then, if the ball goes behind him, it
should hit you if you miss it with your hands; but
always try to collect it with your hands. Do not snatch at
the ball but allow it to run on into your two open hands,
which then close round it. As soon as the ball is in your
hands, get into the habit of moving them towards the
stumps as if you were going to knock off the bails; but
do not touch the stumps or bails unless there is real
justification. If you are standing back for a fast bowler,
run up to the wicket every time the batsman strikes the
ball. At the same time try to get as much practice as
possible in catching the ball by encouraging your fielders
to throw their returns full pitch to your end; and always
take the ball *behind* the stumps, thus giving it a chance
to hit the wicket if it will normally do so. A final hint—
never have a long stop, but rather consider it an insult
if your captain places a fielder there.

Advice for established wicket-keepers

While proficiency only comes as the result of practice
and experience, there are a few fundamental rules for
good wicket-keeping which you will see obeyed by almost
all first-class players; here are some of them:

1. Take every possible ball with two hands, with the
fingers pointing downwards and never towards the

direction of the approaching ball. When the ball arrives higher than the top of the stumps, the elbows have to be bent in order to raise the height of the wrists and thus allow the hands to assume the downward position. When the ball comes as far up as your face, you should point the right hand out towards the off side and at the same time bring the left hand up underneath it.

2. Never snatch at the ball; just allow it to come into the open cup made by your two hands, which then close round the ball. Allow the hands to 'give' just a few inches, bending back slightly at the wrists.

3. Keep your feet as firm as possible; try to avoid moving either, but if necessary move only one, the right one for balls wide of the off stump and the left for balls on the leg side. Beginners are usually 'allowed' to move both

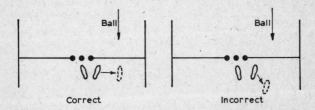

Correct   Incorrect

feet to cover balls on the leg side. When the feet are moved, they must only go sideways, never backwards.

4. Stand as close as possible to the wicket—'nose on the bails' is a well-known slogan—except when the pace makes it advisable to stand back; in that case, stand right back, so as to take the ball on the long hop.

Equipment

No wicket-keeper can do himself justice if his gloves or pads are not comfortable or do not give him the pro-

tection to which he is entitled. Gloves should be large
enough to allow at least one or even two pairs of inners.
Additional protection can be obtained by having pieces
of plasticine on the hand between the palm and the
fingers. There are various forms of 'finish' for the
outer gloves, but each requires some proper attention.
Gloves which are not treated with respect soon become
hard and slippery. Saddler's soap will keep the leather
supple and resin will provide the required slightly sticky
condition; but the addition of tarry material which
comes off the gloves on to the ball in hot weather is not
recommended. Pads should be as wide as possible and
kept specially for wicket-keeping, as they will be too
cumbersome for running when batting.

Catching

If a wicket-keeper takes every ball cleanly, he will
accept nearly all the catches offered, especially if he
takes the ball just behind the bat. The deflection given
to a ball just touched by the edge of a bat is so small that
the position of the hands waiting to take the ball will
also take it when 'snicked'. There is no question of a
wicket-keeper hearing a click and then moving his
hands across just a shade to allow for the deflection; but
when he is standing back the main danger is that, in his
excitement after hearing the click, he will tend to snatch
prematurely at the ball. As is the case with stumping,
it is essential to keep calm and not get flustered. This
applies also when the ball hits the edge of the bat so
firmly that it is deflected in the direction of first slip; in
that case, the wicket-keeper must resist the tendency to
dive across the line of flight of the ball, as such a movement will only obstruct slips' view and probably result
in the catch being missed.

Stumping

It has already been stated that after taking the ball the hands should always be moved in the direction of the stumps, so that, if the batsman's foot moves forward or upwards into the air, the motion can be continued to remove the bails. The most frequent chances of stumping come from slow bowling, and especially from leg-breaks. It is absolutely essential for the wicket-keeper to watch the bowler's hand and so be able to detect his off-break, leg-break, top-spinner or googly. When a chance of stumping seems likely, the hands should take the ball when they have *just* started their forward movement towards the stumps. Remember that you are not allowed to take the ball in front of the wicket—also that you can stump a batsman off a wide. Stumping from balls taken on the leg side is extremely difficult, but you will find that many batsmen—especially rather good ones—are more likely to lift their back foot when trying to score on the leg side than when playing to the off. Occasionally, too, a wicket-keeper can stump a batsman by so moving his left leg to cover a leg-side ball that a rebound on to the wicket off his pad is obtained, although admittedly a good deal of luck is necessary to secure such a decision.

Running out

Just as the wicket-keeper is essential to the bowler for catching and stumping, so is he to the fieldsman who has fielded more adroitly than the batsman anticipated. Except in the few cases when the fielder is lucky enough to throw down the wicket direct, the wicket-keeper must gather the return and at once remove the bails while holding the ball. Most boys manage to break the wicket, but frequently they do so without the ball in hand, and on such occasions many spectators wonder why the umpire did not give the batsman out. The wicket-keeper should stand directly behind the stumps facing the fielder who is about to throw, and he should keep his eye on the ball until it is safely in his hands and *then* move his hands. For a good throw, this movement will be only a matter of inches; for a wide throw, possibly several feet. When fielding practices are being held, a wicket-keeper should be there with proper equipment and a single stump to represent the wickets. As each fielder gathers the ball, he should practise throwing full pitch above the stump straight into the keeper's hands. In this way, you can gain experience in dealing with all sorts of wild throws.

As in the case of stumping, try to keep one foot alongside the wicket and move the other one sideways. For very high throws, you may have to jump off the ground with both feet. Agility is an essential quality of a wicket-keeper; a cool and collected soccer goalkeeper often makes a good cricket stumper. When the throw is such a bad one that it lands at your feet, do not be content with merely stopping it with your pads; try to gather it on the half-volley with your hands and then put the wicket down.

Remember that, if the wicket is thrown down when the batsman is in his ground and the ball rebounds off the stumps, the batsman can take another run. If you have a chance of a run out but both bails are off, you have to pull a stump out of the ground with the hand that holds the ball. A story is told of a rather 'showy' but very determined wicket-keeper who had made up his mind to obtain a wicket in one way if not in another; he took a catch for which he appealed, he put down the wicket with the batsman out of his ground and appealed for stumping, and then, in case neither decision was given in his favour, he pulled up the leg stump and appealed for run out!

Saving the byes

So far nothing has been said about the prevention of
byes, because the main object has been to stress the
aggressive part played by a wicket-keeper in getting out
as many batsmen as possible and in pinning the batsman
down to his ground within the crease. Yet although
byes are of secondary importance, in many junior games
'Mr. Extras' turns out to be the top scorer. If the
fielding side has not many runs to play with, they can ill
afford to allow the wicket-keeper the luxury of several
boundary byes; and in that case, if you have not the
confidence to stop all balls, either because of the bowler's
pace or because so many balls come through on the leg
side, it is much better to stand well back and concentrate
on saving the byes and taking all the catches which are
offered. Even when standing back to fast bowling, you
will have to move quickly whenever a rather wide ball is
sent down, especially if it is on the leg side. First-class
wicket-keepers standing back to the fastest bowlers are
often to be seen diving full length, as if saving a shot
into the corner of a soccer goal.

Finally, if you are interested in keeping records, like
a bowler who finds out from the score book his analysis
in 'runs per wicket', a wicket-keeper can keep his
record in 'byes per wicket', allowing for stumping,
catching and running out. It is partly for that reason
that byes are kept separate from leg byes in the scorebook. Your average should certainly be kept down to
single figures, and as you improve should become less
than five byes per wicket. Try it for a season and see.

CHAPTER 8

Umpiring

Together with the rules of the game of cricket, the
M.C.C. issue 'instructions to umpires'; these refer
mainly to professional umpires of first-class matches.
What follows in this chapter applies more to amateur
umpires, especially to beginners. You will soon find in
your games that most players are willing to take a share
in acting as umpires, and any captain of an eleven is only
too pleased to make use of anyone who is known to be a
reliable umpire. Besides, as already mentioned in the
chapter on batting, one of the best ways of obtaining a
close-up view of the game—and incidentally teaching
yourself—is by acting as an umpire. Because all players
agree to act according to the decisions of the umpires,
it is most important that those decisions should be
correct, and certainly impartial. Correct decisions are,
however, not easy to make, and the advice given here
is mainly for the purpose of helping in that direction.

Let us take an imaginary game from the umpire's
point of view; you may be surprised at the number of
duties he has to perform. First of all, before play begins,
the umpires may be called upon to make a decision when
the conditions of play are doubtful. At the hour due
for the start of the game, the weather may be perfectly
fine, but previously there may have been much rain.
If one captain wishes to play when the other does not,
the umpires are then asked to decide; so they go out
to inspect the wicket and test the softness of the ground.
In most cases, however, the captains agree, so we will

suppose you are told that play will start in a few minutes'
time. Your official dress is a white coat, so that the ball
will show up clearly to the batsmen whenever it travels
in front of the umpire who is standing beside the wicket.

Now, as you will have to count the six balls bowled for
each over, it is a considerable help to have ready in
your pocket six coins or six small stones, and, in order to
avoid a last minute search, you should be prepared with
these before you go out on to the field of play. The
umpires are responsible for taking out the bails and
placing them fairly on the stumps, and it is also their
duty to see that the wickets are properly spaced and
upright; for instance, if a ball will pass between any
two of the stumps, they are too far apart. The umpires
also have to take out the balls, a new one for the game
and spare ones in case the proper ball is hit out of the
ground and lost. Many cricket grounds in all parts of
the country have rivers or woods or built-up areas
adjacent to the playing field, and big hits are often
liable to result in the loss of the ball, at any rate tempora-
rily. It is for such emergencies that at least one spare
ball should always be taken out by the umpires.

You will have come to an agreement with your com-
panion as to which end you will each stand, and it is
the custom that you stay at the same end for the first
innings of both sides; only in a two innings match do the
umpires change ends. Let us suppose you are at the
bowler's end for the first over. Your initial duty is to
ask the player who is about to bowl whether he is right
or left arm, and whether he delivers the ball from over
or round the wicket. The batsman at the other end will
then ask for guard. To give this, you stand directly
behind the stumps and not to one side, unless the batsman asks you specifically to give him the guard from
the outside of the crease or from some other place. If
the batsman wishes to make his block in line with the

middle stump, he will ask for 'middle'; if in line with
the leg stump, he requests 'leg stump' or 'one leg'; if in
between those two positions, he says 'middle and leg' or
'two leg' or 'covering both'. Very few batsmen will ask
for 'off stump' or 'middle and off', although a number
will prefer to take a guard just outside the leg stump. The
umpire is not concerned with *where* the batsman makes
his block; he is merely there in an advisory capacity.

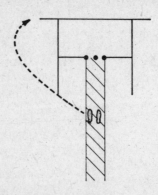

Once you have given the batsman his guard, you then
take up your position behind the line of the stumps and
facing down the wicket. You should not move from this
position after the ball is bowled, and all l.b.w. decisions
have to be given from over the wicket and not from
where the ball has been delivered. The bowler is at
liberty to request you to stand up or back anywhere in
the shaded area in the above diagram, but, unless it
interferes with the bowler's run or arm-swing, a
position 2 or 3 yards behind the wicket is the best for all
practical purposes. If there is a chance of a player being
run out at your end of the pitch, you should move quickly
in the direction of the arrow so as to place yourself in the
best position to answer such an appeal.

As soon as the fielding side and the batsmen are ready, you call 'play', and the game begins. As each ball is bowled, you must see that it is a fair ball; needless to say, the ball must be *bowled*, not thrown or jerked, but your main task is to watch the bowler's feet. In the delivery stride part of the bowler's front foot must be grounded behind the popping crease, and his back foot must land within and not touching the return crease or its forward extension. If these conditions are not fulfilled, as in the two cases of the diagrams below, you must call immediately in a loud voice 'no ball', and then signal the information to the scorers by holding out your right arm in a horizontal position.

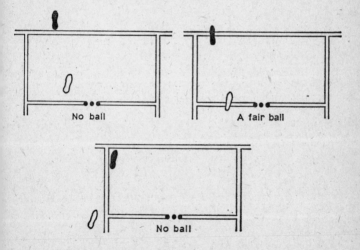

It is most important for the umpire to call 'no ball' loudly, clearly and immediately, so that all the players may realize that this is a special kind of ball. The batsman particularly wants to know at the earliest possible second, so that he can hit out at the ball with the knowledge that he cannot be bowled or caught or stumped. It is, in fact, a 'free' ball to him only if he receives due notice of it, and, in the case of fast bowlers especially, this calls for great speed of thought and action on the part of the umpire.

If a ball is bowled so high over or so wide of the wicket that in your opinion it is not within range of the striker, you shall call 'wide ball' and signal to the scorers by holding both arms out in a horizontal position. Note the definition of the 'wide'. Many players think that a ball must be a wide if it passes outside the return crease; that is not so, although in practice it is the *average* limiting position. However, a ball might be a wide to a small boy yet not to a tall grown-up player, because the young boy might not be able to reach a ball that the other batsman could. Also, if a ball is outside the line of the return crease and the batsman, by moving his feet and arms, swings his bat below or above the ball, he 'covers' that ball and therefore reaches it—and no wide should be given. Incidentally, an umpire should bear in mind that no balls and wides do not count in the over.

As each good ball is bowled, the umpire should pass a coin or stone from one hand to the other or into a pocket. In an uneventful over, it is easy enough to count six balls; but supposing that three runs are scored from the first ball and there is an appeal for a run out, then a no-ball is bowled, followed by some more runs and then a wicket; by the time the new batsman has arrived at the crease, you will have become confused unless you have adopted some definite system of counting. Be careful not to call 'over' after the sixth good ball until the ball is settled in the bowler's or wicket-keeper's hands, or until it is stationary so near the wicket that no run is possible. In addition to the signalling of no balls and wides, you have also to signal for byes, leg byes, short runs, boundaries and sizes, so that the scorers, however far away they may be, know exactly what is happening. The standard signals are:

Bye: The hand held above the head.

Leg bye: The hand held above the head and one foot raised.

Short run: One arm bent upwards and over to touch the shoulder with the tips of the fingers; also call 'one short run' so that everybody may know.

Boundary: The arm waved from side to side in front of you in four movements.

Six (a full pitch over the boundary): Raise both arms above the head.

These signals should be known by all players and prospective umpires, because it is possible, though highly improbable, that they all might be used in one over.

Let us now assume that six good balls have been delivered by the bowler at your end; when you have called 'over', go to the square-leg position, and from about 15 to 20 yards away from the wicket be ready to give decisions on appeals for 'run out' and 'stumped'. At the same time look out for short runs whenever the batsman does not ground his bat *over* the line as he turns for each run. The other umpire, at the bowler's end, has the task of counting the balls now. If there is a left-handed batsman playing, you will get some exercise, because, just as the square-leg fielding position alters from one side of the wicket to the other, the umpire must cross over, too. If there is any good reason, such as the sun shining in your eyes, the square-leg umpire may obtain permission from the captain of the fielding side to remain in his position on one side of the wicket.

During your position at the wicket, you have to be ready to answer appeals for 'l.b.w.' and 'caught at the wicket'. These decisions are sometimes easy, sometimes hard. Whenever there is a real doubt, the batsman should have the benefit and be given 'not out'. According to the present rules of cricket (which do not include any experimental laws that may be being tried out), all the following conditions must be fulfilled for you to give a player out under the l.b.w. rule:

1. It must be a good ball—that is, not a no ball.
2. The ball must have pitched on the line of the wicket or on the off side.
3. The ball must be going on to hit the wicket and not over the top of the stumps.
4. The ball must hit the pad or leg of the player without having previously been hit or snicked by his bat.
5. The position of the pad or leg or foot, when hit by the ball, must be in the line of the wicket.

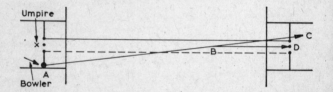

Observe now from the above diagram how difficult it is for a right-hand bowler who is bowling *round* the wicket to get a batsman l.b.w. unless he bowls off-breaks. A ball bowled from the point of delivery at A must pitch on the left side of the dotted line if an l.b.w. decision is to be obtained, so you can see that it must reach the batsman well pitched up. If such a ball did not 'straighten out' by means of an off-break at B to D it would pass the wicket wide of the off stump towards C, and the l.b.w. appeal would for that reason be negatived. Finally, note that, if you are in doubt, you cannot refer to your fellow umpire but must say 'not out'.

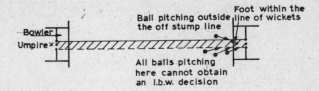

As each ball is bowled, you should therefore concentrate on seeing whether it pitches outside the line between the leg stumps—the line of dots in the diagram. If it *is* outside, any l.b.w. appeal must be answered 'not out'. When a ball hits a player, you should notice at once whether that place of contact is between the two lines in the figure, and at the same time judge if the ball would have gone on to hit the stumps. Then, finally, before giving a batsman out, say to yourself 'Did he hit the ball with his bat?' The figure illustrates how it is possible for an off-break to get a right-handed player l.b.w., but under the present rules a corresponding leg-break cannot do so.

Now for the appeal 'How's that?' when the wicket-keeper or first slip catches a ball after there has been an audible click as the ball passed the batsman. The important point here is that you must have seen the ball in contact with the edge of the bat. Clicks can be made by a variety of causes such as the straps of the pads, the ball hitting the clothing and the bat striking against a pad or boot. You should be satisfied that at the moment when there was a click the ball was so near to the bat that it must have been in contact with it; in most cases, a slight change in the direction of the ball will be seen. Incidentally, a player is out caught off his hand or glove but not off his wrist or arm. In the case of a bowler who follows on up the wicket with the result that he completely blocks your view, you should warn him of the fact, and in the case of an appeal you must say 'not out'. In all cases, do not be influenced by the noise made by the fielding side; a quiet appeal made by the bowler alone must be given just as much consideration as a general chorus from all the eleven fielders.

Let us now imagine that you are back again at square-leg and the batsman, attempting a drive, misses the ball; the wicket-keeper whips off the bails with a cry of 'how's that?' Again you must go through several points in your mind:

1. Did the wicket-keeper allow the ball to pass the wicket before taking it?

2. Did the wicket-keeper break the wicket with his hands *while holding the ball*?

3. At the moment when the wicket was broken was the batsman out of his crease? Remember in that connection that 'on the line is out'. For a batsman to be in his crease part of his foot or his bat must be grounded *behind* the white line.

Except for point No. 1 above, the same conditions apply to a 'run out' decision. You must be particularly careful to be sure that the person at the wicket has the ball in his hand when the wicket is broken; so often, in his excitement, the player will half-catch the ball and then move some part of his body which knocks off the bails. Also be sure that when a batsman reaches out with his bat in front of him, the bat is running along the ground and not in the air.

Having returned to the wicket at the end of another over, the umpire, we will now imagine, has to deal with some less familiar appeals. For instance, after a batsman has hooked a ball round to leg, the bails of his wicket are seen to be on the ground and there is an appeal for 'How's that—hit wicket?' The rule says that, if, in playing at the ball, the batsman hits his wicket with his

bat or any part of his person or dress, he is out. If you
are not in a position to say whether that was the case,
you should then ask the square-leg umpire to decide.
Later on in the same over, the batsman plays a ball just
off the ground and it is caught; the fielder appeals for a
catch. You then have to decide whether the ball followed course A ('bumped ball') or course B (catch)
after it was struck. Such a decision seems easy enough
to make, but on a hard ground it is often a difficult
problem when the ball is struck with the bottom of the
bat.

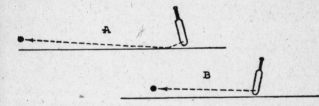

Later in the over you give a 'no ball', and, with the
wicket-keeper failing to stop the ball, it runs behind him
and the batsmen take two runs. You merely signal the
no ball and the scorers record *two* no balls and no byes.
The same rule applies to any runs taken after a wide is
given. As each new batsman comes in, remember that he
will require to be given guard, and it is usual to tell him
how many more balls are due to be bowled in that over.
Your remarks will take some such form as this: 'one leg'
—he moves his bat towards the off; 'centre'—he moves
his bat a little nearer towards his body; 'two leg'—he
makes his block and glances round the field; 'three balls
to come'—he takes up his stance and prepares to receive
his first ball.

Yet another function of the umpires is to act as time-
keepers for the stopping of play for an interval or at the
close of play. If both of you have watches, you should

synchronize them when play is about to start. When there is less than two minutes before the agreed time for the end of play, one of the umpires should inform the players that they are about to begin the 'last over'. According to the rules, as altered in 1947, once the last over has started, either captain may demand that it must be finished, no matter how much time is taken up by the fall of wickets.

When play ceases before an interval, it is usual for the umpires to remove the bails, and at the end of the day's play they often assist the groundsmen—if any—by bringing in the stumps. When you have returned the balls and your umpire's coat, your duties are finished. You may not feel completely satisfied with all your decisions, but if you have acted impartially and done your best to deal with any difficult cases you will at any rate have earned the thanks of the players.

Most of the normal problems which beset an umpire have now been covered, but all sorts of unexpected things happen in cricket. One result of this is that the umpire, especially in village cricket, has become the subject of many amusing stories. Perhaps a suitable ending for this chapter is the description of the exciting finish between two rival village cricket elevens. One side required only two runs for a win when their stalwart No. 11 batsman took a terrific swipe at the first ball he received. There was a dull thud as the ball hit him smartly on the pad, a roar of 'how's that?' from dozens of throats and a quiet response from the white-coated 'neutral' figure at the other end of the pitch—'Out! We've won!'

PROBLEMS FOR UMPIRES

1. In the action of bowling, the bowler knocks both bails off the wicket.

(*a*) Should you give a no ball?

(*b*) Should you replace the bails at once?

(*c*) Can a batsman be run out without the bails being on the wicket?

2. After you have called 'over', one of the fielders makes an appeal for a catch at the wicket off the last ball of the over. Is his appeal too late to be considered?

3. One of the balls of an over is a no ball, from which the batsman scores a run. Should that ball count as one of the six for the over?

4. Can a batsman be stumped off a wide?

5. A batsman clearly snicks a ball and the wicket-keeper misses the catch, but the ball drops into the top of his pads and stays there. Should you give the batsman out?

6. A batsman allows a ball to roll on to his wicket which is hit by the ball, but not hard enough to knock off a bail. Is the player bowled?

7. A batsman hits the ball straight back and knocks down the opposite wicket when his partner is backing up out of his crease. Is that player run out?

8. Is a bowler allowed to change his method of bowling (for example, from 'over' to 'round' the wicket) in the middle of an over?

9. Can a batsman be caught by a fielder leaning against a boundary fence:

(*a*) If the ball is not beyond the perpendicular above the boundary fence?

(*b*) If the ball is beyond the perpendicular?

10. A batsman jumps out of his ground and misses the ball, which rebounds from the wicket-keeper's pads and knocks off the bails. Is the batsman out, and, if so, how?

Answers

1. (a) No.
   (b) No.
   (c) Yes; if both bails are off, a stump must be pulled out of the ground while the ball is held in the same hand.

2. No. An appeal can be made for an incident arising out of the last ball of an over any time before the first ball of the next over has been delivered.

3. No.

4. Yes (Law 29).

5. Yes (Law 35, Note 4).

6. If you have definitely observed the bail to be dislodged and then come back or become wedged, the batsman is out 'bowled'; otherwise he is not out.

7. No, not unless the ball has been touched by a fielder on its way to the wicket.

8. Yes—provided that the umpire and the batsman are informed.

9. Yes—he is caught in both cases.

10. Yes—stumped.

CHAPTER 9

Learning the Game by Scoring

Each cricket eleven usually has its official scorer, but on many occasions a scorer may be required at the last moment and one of the players frequently takes on the job while his side is batting. Like so many things in life, scoring is easy to do in a rough and ready way, but it is not so easy to do it really well, especially when runs are being scored rapidly. All the same, one of the best ways of approaching the game is to act as an amateur scorer, and thousands of youngsters obtain their initial keenness for cricket through the medium of a sheet of paper or scorecard or scorebook. Since a great deal can be learned from scoring, let us now keep a scorebook for an imaginary game; here is a small portion of it:

	NAME	RUNS	HOW OUT	BOWLER	TOTAL
1.	Jones	2·1·3·1	RUN	OUT	7
2.	Brown	1·	BOWLED	SMITH	1
3.	Robinson	1·2·4·			

Byes					
Leg Byes					
Wides	1·				
No-Balls	1·				

						WIDES	NO-BALLS
1. Williams						1·	1·
2. Smith							
3. Johnson							

Let us now describe the happenings which led to the above short extract from the page of a scorebook. The opening bowler—Williams—was fast-medium; his first ball was on the off side and was allowed to go through to the wicket-keeper, so a dot is put down in the bowling analysis. The second ball is played but no run is taken; another dot goes down. The third ball is placed to leg for two; two is placed in the analysis and a two with a dot following it is placed along the batsman's line as a credit to Jones; at the same time, two runs are marked off the 'total' record. The fourth ball is a 'no ball', which the umpire signals with his outstretched arm; the batsman swings at the ball but misses. A dot with a cross above it is placed in the analysis and further along a single goes in the 'no ball' column, in addition to a single in the 'no ball' line of 'extras', while the 'total' is now marked as three. The next ball is placed by Jones for a single; one in the bowling analysis; one for the batsman; four for the total. No run is scored from the sixth ball, Brown's first, but because of the no ball there is a seventh ball in this over, and from it Brown scores a single. This is recorded in between the third and sixth balls in the analysis; Brown is credited with his one run, and the total becomes five. As this is the end of the over, the total number of runs scored off the bowler is written thus, ④ at the top of the rectangle, and if you have a colleague scoring with you, you now check the 'extras' and the scores of each batsman.

By this time, the bowler from the other end—Smith— has bowled his first ball, from which there is no score; the second is the same, so two dots go down in the analysis. To the third ball Brown attempts a late cut, but he unluckily snicks the ball on to his wicket. This is generally referred to as 'playing on', but 'bowled' is the official term for the 'how out' column. In the analysis a small 'w' is recorded for the wicket; make an oblique

stroke after the 'one' of the batsman's runs so as to
prevent you crediting him with any more runs by
mistake; fill in 'bowled' and the bowler's name (Smith),
and insert his total (one) at the end of the line. Then
place the total (five) for the first wicket in the space
provided and, if there is a space below for the number of
the out-going batsman, insert 'two' there.

Play will have again re-started and batsman No. 3,
Robinson, plays out the rest of Smith's over without
incident. The over is therefore a 'wicket maiden'
because no run was scored; it is accordingly marked
with a large 'W'. The details are agreed by your com-
panion to be the same as before, and the fast bowler,
Williams, resumes at the other end. The second ball is
cut for three; for the fourth ball a wide is signalled, and,
as the wicket-keeper fails to gather it on the leg side,
the batsmen run one run as it goes down towards fine-leg.
This is an occasion where many scorers and onlookers
go wrong. The run taken by the batsmen was quite
unnecessary, since the score is just one wide. In the
analysis, a dot with a circle above it is put down, also a
single in the column for the bowler's wides. Then a
single is placed in the 'wides' line of 'extras' and the
total is marked off to nine. The fifth and sixth balls each
give the batsmen a single and the extra ball, for the wide,
results in no score. Williams has now had a total of nine
runs scored off his first two overs from the bat—wides
and no balls do not count in the analysis—so we put ⑨
above his second over.

After the customary check with the other scorer, we
are ready for the next over. Two runs are scored off
Smith's first ball, and then, after three good length balls,
a full toss is sent down and is properly hit by Robinson
to the boundary; we acknowledge the umpires' signal
as we did previously for the no ball and wide. The last
ball of the over is also over-pitched and is hit to cover

point; the batsmen start to run, but the ball is brilliantly fielded and returned to the wicket-keeper before Jones can reach his crease and he is run out. A dot goes down in the analysis, because the bowler received no credit for a run out. The same procedure is carried out as when the previous wicket fell. The total is now seventeen for two wickets, and the out-going batsman is No. 1.

In spite of the fielding side's success, there is a change of bowling, so in the space for the opening bowler's third over we place a cross, indicating the end of his spell, and ⑨ is written for the total runs scored as the result of his bowling so far. Batsman No. 3, Robinson, is now content to play a maiden over from Johnson, the new bowler; so over the six dots an 'M' is marked.

The above few overs have illustrated sufficiently the main routine work of a scorer. Routine is the essential point; there is a definite routine after every ball, after every over and after every wicket. After every ball, the bowling analysis should be marked first, next the runs—if any—to the batsman or 'extras', and then the total. After every over, add up the runs scored off the bowler, record the total to date and check up with your colleague. After every wicket, add up totals and check with bowling analysis totals and 'extras'.

As a summary on this subject of scoring, here are four key questions, with their answers:

1. The umpire signals a wide, but the wicket-keeper fails to stop the ball which goes to the boundary. What is scored? [*Ans.* = Four wides.]

2. The umpire signals a no ball, but the batsman plays the ball and takes one run. What is scored? [*Ans.* = One run to the batsman only.]

3. One batsman drives the ball to long-on, takes one run but in trying for a second run, he is run out. What is scored? [*Ans.* = One run to striker.]

4. A batsman hits a ball very high into the deep, calls for a run and reaches the other crease just before the ball is caught near the boundary. What is scored? [*Ans.* = No score.]

Other Methods of Scoring

If you are not keeping the official scorebook for a game, there are several ways in which you can keep a partial record of the play. These are usually done for the sake of amusement or interest, perhaps just for a few players who happen to be your particular favourites.

If you fill in the scores of all the batsmen but prefer to omit the bowling analysis, the inclusion of a number of clock times lends additional interest. For instance, you can put down the time when the innings started, and afterwards note the number of overs bowled in each hour and the number of balls received by each batsman. This will enable you to calculate his rate of scoring. Whenever a batsman is given a life by a missed catch, a cross can be placed along his record of runs. Again, when you think he has scored any runs by a lucky stroke, as, for example, an intended cover drive which scores four through the slips, you can put a ring round the figure, thus ④. All such records give added interest and are specially suitable for inserting on the match-cards sold at all county matches.

Stroke charts

Finally, if you take a blank sheet of paper, a pencil and a ruler, you can keep a record of every scoring stroke made by a batsman. You merely draw the wicket in plan in the centre of your sheet and insert lines showing the direction and distance travelled by the ball. By drawing concentric circles representing one, two, three

and four runs each, the value of every scoring stroke
can be represented. If you want the correct order, a
series of letters, *a, b, c, d* . . ., can be placed at the end of
each line, and, in addition, the above-mentioned system
of crosses for chances and rings for lucky shots can give
almost a complete story of a player's innings. Here is an
example from which a full reconstruction of an innings
can be made:

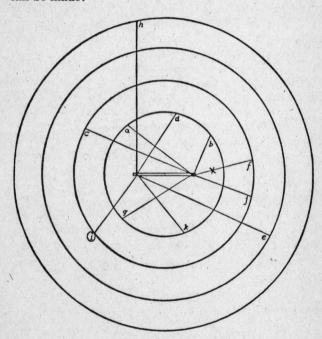

RUN CHART FOR AN INNINGS OF 20

The Laws of Cricket

(1947 Code—4th Edition)

OFFICIAL

London
Marylebone Cricket Club
1968,
incorporating amendments
May 1969 and May 1971

World Copyright Reserved

PREFACE

During the last two hundred years the conduct of the game of Cricket has been governed by a series of Codes of Laws. These Codes were established as indicated below and were at all times subject to additions and alterations ordained by the governing authorities of the time. Since its formation in 1787 the Marylebone Cricket Club has been recognized as the sole authority for drawing up the Code and for all subsequent alterations.

There is little doubt that Cricket was subject to recognized rules as early as 1700, though the earliest known Code is that drawn up in 1744 by certain Noblemen and Gentlemen who used the Artillery Ground in London. These Laws were revised in 1755 by 'Several Cricket Clubs, particularly that of the Star and Garter in Pall Mall'.

The next arrangement was produced by 'a Committee of Noblemen and Gentlemen of Kent, Hampshire, Surrey, Sussex, Middlesex and London,' at the Star and Garter on February 25th, 1774, and this in turn was revised by a similar body in February, 1786.

On May 30th, 1788, the first M.C.C. Code was adopted, and remained in force until May 19th, 1835, when a new Code of Laws was approved by the Committee. The Laws appear to have been first numbered in 1823.

The 1835 Code, amended in detail from time to time, stood until April 21st, 1884, when, after consultation with cricket clubs both at home and overseas, important alterations were incorporated in a new version adopted at a Special General Meeting of the M.C.C.

By 1939, these Laws supplemented as they had been by the inclusion of many definitions and interpretations in the form of notes, were in need of revision, and immediately on the conclusion of the World War the opinions of controlling Bodies and Clubs throughout the world were sought, with the result that the present code was adopted at a Special General Meeting of the M.C.C. on May 7th, 1947.

This revision in the main aimed at the clarification and better arrangement of the previous Laws and their interpretations, but did not exclude certain definite alterations designed firstly to provide greater latitude in the conduct of the game as required by the widely differing conditions in which it is played, and secondly to eliminate certain umpiring difficulties.

This, the fourth edition of the 1947 Code, contains a few small alterations to the Laws and certain alterations and amendments to the Notes published since 1962.

Under the Rules of the Marylebone Cricket Club the Laws of Cricket can only be changed by the vote of two-thirds of the members present and voting at a Special General Meeting, of which due notice is required to be given.

From time to time the Committee of the M.C.C. are required to give interpretations on points of difficulty arising from the Laws, and these are given in the form of notes to the Laws themselves.

The primary purpose of the book as expressed by the late Sir Francis Lacey (Secretary of the M.C.C. from 1898 to 1926) remains unchanged:

'The aim of this publication is to remove difficulties, which are known to exist, although they are not always apparent. Hundreds of cases are sent to the M.C.C. for decision every year. It is from this source that the chief difficulties have become manifest. Saturday and League

Matches are especially productive of disputes, and it is hoped that those who read these notes may find an answer to any doubt which may arise as to the proper interpretation of the Laws of Cricket.'

Lord's Cricket Ground,
   London, N.W.8.   S. C. GRIFFITH,
1st June, 1968.   Secretary, M.C.C.

CONTENTS

THE LAWS OF CRICKET

The term 'Special Regulations' referred to in certain Laws are those authorised by M.C.C., Overseas Governing Bodies or other Cricket Authorities in respect of matches played under their jurisdiction.

(A) THE PLAYERS, UMPIRES AND SCORERS

1. A match is played between two sides of eleven players each, unless otherwise agreed. Each side shall play under a Captain who before the toss for innings shall nominate his players who may not thereafter be changed without the consent of the opposing Captain.

NOTES

1. If a captain is not available at any time, a deputy must act for him to deal promptly with points arising from this and other Laws.

2. No match in which more than eleven players a side take part can be regarded as First-class, and in any case no side should field with more than eleven players.

SUBSTITUTES

2. Substitutes shall be allowed to field or run between the wickets for any player who may during the match be incapacitated from illness or injury, but not for any other reason without the consent of the opposing Captain; no Substitute shall be allowed to bat or to bowl. Consent as to

the person to act as substitute in the field shall be
obtained from the opposing Captain, who may
indicate positions in which the Substitute shall not
field.

NOTES

1. A player may bat, bowl or field even though a substitute has acted for him previously.

2. An injured batsman may be 'Out' should his runner
infringe Laws 36, 40 or 41. As *Striker* he remains himself
subject to the Laws; should he be out of his ground for
any purpose he may be 'Out' under Laws 41 and 42 at
the wicket-keeper's end, irrespective of the position of the
other batsman or the substitute when the wicket is put
down. When *not the Striker* the injured batsman is out of
the game and stands where he does not interfere with the
play.

THE APPOINTMENT OF UMPIRES

3. Before the toss for innings two Umpires shall
be appointed one for each end to control the game
as required by the Laws with absolute impartial-
ity. No Umpire shall be changed during a match
without the consent of both Captains.

NOTE

1. The umpires should report themselves to the
executive of the ground 30 minutes before the start of
each day's play.

THE SCORERS

4. All runs scored shall be recorded by Scorers
appointed for the purpose; the Scorers shall accept
and acknowledge all instructions and signals given
to them by the Umpires.

NOTE

1. The umpires should wait until a signal has been answered by a scorer before allowing the game to proceed. Mutual consultation between the scorers and the umpires to clear up doubtful points is at all times permissible.

(B) THE IMPLEMENTS OF THE GAME, AND THE GROUND

THE BALL

5. The ball shall weigh not less than $5\frac{1}{2}$ ounces, not more than $5\frac{3}{4}$ ounces. It shall measure not less than $8\frac{13}{16}$ inches, nor more than 9 inches in circumference. Subject to agreement to the contrary either Captain may demand a new ball at the start of each innings. In the event of a ball being lost or becoming unfit for play, the Umpires shall allow another ball to be taken into use. They shall inform the Batsmen whenever a ball is to be changed.

NOTES

1. All cricket balls used in First-class matches should be approved before the start of a match by the umpires and captains.

2. In First-class matches, the Captain of the fielding side may demand a new ball after the prescribed number of overs has been bowled with the old one. The Governing Body for cricket in the country concerned shall decide the number of overs applicable in that country, which shall be not less than 75 overs, nor more than 85 overs (55 to 65 eight ball overs).

In other grades of cricket, these regulations will not apply unless agreed before the toss for innings.

3. Any ball substituted for one lost or becoming unfit for play should have had similar wear or use as that of the one discarded.

THE BAT

6. The Bat shall not exceed $4\frac{1}{4}$ inches in the widest part; it shall not be more than 38 inches in length.

THE PITCH

7. The Pitch is deemed to be the area of ground between the bowling creases, 5 feet in width on either side of the line joining the centre of the wickets. Before the toss for innings, the executive of the ground shall be responsible for the selection and preparation of the Pitch; thereafter the Umpires shall control its use and maintenance. The Pitch shall not be changed during a match unless it becomes unfit for play, and then only with the consent of both Captains.

THE WICKETS

8. The Wickets shall be pitched opposite and parallel to each other at a distance of 22 yards from stump to stump. Each Wicket shall be 9 inches in width and consist of three stumps with two bails upon the top. The stumps shall be of equal and or sufficient size to prevent the ball from passing through, with their top 28 inches above the ground. The bails shall be each $4\frac{3}{8}$ inches in length and, when in position on the top of the stumps, shall not project more than $\frac{1}{2}$ inch above them.

NOTES

1. Except for the bail grooves the tops of the stumps shall be dome-shaped.

2. In a high wind the captains may agree, with the approval of the umpires, to dispense with the use of bails. (*See* Law 31, Note 3.)

THE BOWLING AND POPPING CREASES

9. The bowling crease shall be marked in line with the stumps: 8 feet 8 inches (2·64 m) in length; with the stumps in the centre. The popping crease shall be marked 4 feet (1·22 m) in front of and parallel with the popping crease and shall extend a minimum of 6 feet (1·83 m) either side of the line of the stumps. The return crease shall be marked at each end of the bowling crease, at right angles to it, and shall extend forward to join the popping crease, and a minimum of 4 feet (1·22 m) behind the wicket. Both the return and popping creases shall be deemed unlimited in length.

NOTES

1. The distance of the popping crease from the wicket is measured from a line running through the centre of the stumps to the inside edge of the crease.

2. Whenever possible, the popping crease and the return crease shall be redrawn during each interval.

(C) THE CARE AND MAINTENANCE OF THE PITCH

ROLLING, MOWING AND WATERING

10. Unless permitted by 'Special Regulations', the Pitch shall not be rolled during a match except

before the start of each innings and of each day's play, when, if the Captain of the batting side so elect, it may be swept and rolled for not more than 7 minutes. In a match of less than three days' duration, the pitch shall not be mown during the match unless 'Special Regulations' so provide. In a match of three or more days' duration, the pitch shall be mown under the supervision of the Umpires before play begins on alternate days after the start of a match, but should the pitch not be so mown on any day on account of play not taking place, it shall be mown on the first day on which the match is resumed and thereafter on alternate days. (For the purpose of this Law a rest day counts as a day.) Under no circumstances shall the Pitch be watered during a match.

NOTES

1. The umpires are responsible that any rolling permitted by this Law and carried out at the request of the captain of the batting side is in accordance with the regulations laid down and that it is completed so as to allow play to start at the stipulated time.

The normal rolling before the start of each day's play shall take place not earlier than half an hour before the start of play, but the captain of the batting side may delay such rolling until 10 minutes before the start of play should he so desire.

2. The time allowed for rolling shall be taken out of the normal playing time if a captain declare an innings closed either, (a) before play starts on any day so late that the other captain is prevented from exercising his option in regard to rolling under this Law, or (b) during the luncheon interval later than 15 minutes after the start of such interval.

3. Except in the United Kingdom, if at any time a rain

affected pitch is damaged by play thereon, it shall be swept and rolled for a period of not more than ten consecutive minutes at any time between the close of play on the day on which it was damaged and the next resumption of play, provided that:

(i) The umpires shall instruct the groundsman to sweep and roll the pitch only after they have agreed that damage caused to it as a result of play after rain has fallen warrants such rolling additional to that provided for in Law 10.

(ii) Such rolling shall in all cases be done under the personal supervision of both umpires and shall take place at such time and with such roller as the groundsman shall consider best calculated to repair the damage to the pitch.

(iii) Not more than one such additional rolling shall be permitted as a result of rain on any particular day.

(iv) The rolling provided for in Law 10, to take place before the start of play, shall not be permitted on any day on which the rolling herein provided for takes place within two hours of the time appointed for commencement of the play on that day.

COVERING THE PITCH

11. The Pitch shall not be completely covered during a match unless 'Special Regulations' so provide; covers used to protect the bowlers' run up shall not extend to a greater distance than $3\frac{1}{2}$ feet in front of the Popping creases.

NOTE

1. It is usual under this Law to protect the bowlers' run up, before and during a match, both at night and,

when necessary, during the day. The covers should be removed early each morning, if fine.

MAINTENANCE OF THE PITCH

12. The Batsman may beat the Pitch with his bat, and Players may secure their footholds by the use of sawdust, provided Law 46 be not thereby contravened. In wet weather the Umpires shall see that the holes made by the Bowlers and Batsmen are cleaned out and dried whenever necessary to facilitate play.

(D) THE CONDUCT OF THE GAME

INNINGS

13. Each side has two innings, taken alternately, except the case provided for in Law 14. The choice of innings shall be decided by tossing on the field of play.

NOTES

1. The captains should toss for innings not later than 15 minutes before the time agreed upon for play to start. The winner of the toss may not alter his decision to bat or field once it has been notified to the opposing captain.

2. This Law also governs a One-day match in which play continues after the completion of the first innings of both sides. (*See also* Law 22.)

FOLLOWING INNINGS

14. The side which bats first and leads by 200 runs in a match of five days or more, by 150 runs in a three-day or four-day match, by 100 runs in a

two-day match or by 75 runs in a one-day match, shall have the option of requiring the other side to follow their innings.

DECLARATIONS

15. The Captain of the batting side may declare an innings closed at any time during a match irrespective of its duration.

NOTE

1. A captain may forfeit his second innings. In this event, the interval between innings shall be 10 minutes and his decision must be notified to the opposing captain and umpires in sufficient time to allow seven minutes rolling of the pitch.

16. When the start of play is delayed by weather Law 14 shall apply in accordance with the number of days' play remaining from the actual start of the match.

START AND CLOSE OF PLAY AND INTERVALS

17. The Umpires shall allow such intervals as have been agreed upon for meals, 10 minutes between each innings and not more than 2 minutes for each fresh batsman to come in. At the start of each innings and of each day's play and at the end of any interval the Umpire at the Bowler's end shall call 'Play' when the side refusing to play shall lose the match. After 'Play' has been called no trial ball shall be allowed to any player, and when one of the Batsman is out the use of the bat shall not be allowed to any player until the next Batsman shall come in.

NOTES

1. The umpires shall not award a match under this Law unless (i) 'Play' has been called in such a manner that both sides can clearly understand that play is to start, (ii) an appeal has been made, and (iii) they are satisfied that a side will not, or cannot, continue play.

2. It is an essential duty of the captains to ensure that the 'in-going' batsman passes the 'out-coming' one before the latter leaves the field of play. This is all the more important in view of the responsibility resting on the umpires for deciding whether or not the delay of the individual amounts to a refusal of the batting side to continue play.

3. The interval for luncheon should not exceed 45 minutes unless otherwise agreed (but *see* Law 10, Note 2). In the event of the last wicket falling within 2 minutes of the time arranged for luncheon or tea, the game shall be resumed at the usual hour, no allowance being made for the 10 minutes between the innings.

4. Bowling practice *on the pitch* is forbidden at any time during the game.

18. The Umpires shall call 'Time' and at the same time remove the bails from both wickets, on the cessation of play before any arranged interval, at the end of each day's play, and at the conclusion of the match. An 'Over' shall always be started if 'Time' has not been reached, and shall be completed unless a batsman is 'Out' or 'Retires' within 2 minutes of the completion of any period of play, but the 'Over' in progress at the close of play on the final day of a match shall be completed at the request of either Captain even if a wicket fall after 'Time' has been reached.

NOTES

1. If, during the completion of the last over of any period of play, the players have occasion to leave the field, the Umpires shall call 'time'. In the case of the last over of the match, there shall be no resumption of play and the match shall be at an end.

2. The last over before an interval or the close of play shall be started, provided the umpire standing at square leg, after walking at his normal pace, has arrived at his position behind the stumps at the bowler's end before time has been reached. The above provision will apply if the batsman is 'Out' off, or 'Retires' after the last ball of an over when less than two minutes remain for play at the conclusion of the match.

SCORING

19. The score shall be reckoned by runs. A run is scored:

1st.—So often as the Batsman after a hit, or at any time while the ball is in play, shall have crossed and made good their ground from end to end; but if either Batsman run a short run, the Umpire shall call and signal 'One short' and that run shall not be scored. The Striker being caught, no run shall be scored; a Batsman being run out, that run which was being attempted shall not be scored.

2nd.—For penalties under Laws 21, 27, 29, 44 and boundary allowances under Law 20.

NOTES

1. If while the ball is in play, the batsman have crossed in running, neither returns to the wicket he has left except in the case of a boundary hit, or a boundary from

extras, or under Laws 30 Note 1 and 46 Note 4 (vii). This rule applies even should a short run have been called, or should no run be reckoned as in the case of a catch.

2. A run is 'short' if either or both batsmen fail to make good their ground in turning for a further run.

Although such a 'short' run shortens the succeeding one, the latter, if completed, counts. Similarly a batsman taking stance in front of his popping crease may run from that point without penalty.

3. (i) One run only is deducted if both batsmen are short in one and the same run.

(ii) Only if three or more runs are attempted can more than one run be 'short' and then, subject to (i) above, all runs so called shall be disallowed.

(iii) If either or both batsmen deliberately run short, the umpire is justified in calling 'Dead Ball' and disallowing any runs attempted or scored as soon as he sees that the fielding side have no chance of dismissing either batsman under the Laws.

4. An umpire signals 'short' runs when the ball becomes 'dead' by bending his arm upwards to touch the shoulder with the tips of his fingers. If there has been more than one 'short' run the umpires must instruct the scorers as to the number of runs disallowed. (*See* Note 1 to Law 4.)

BOUNDARIES

20. Before the toss for innings the Umpires shall agree with both sides on the Boundaries for play, and on the allowances to be made for them. An Umpire shall call or signal 'Boundary' whenever, in his opinion, a ball in play hits, crosses or is carried over the Boundary. The runs completed at the instant the ball reaches the Boundary shall only count should they exceed the allowance, but if

the 'Boundary' result from an overthrow or from the wilful act of a fieldsman, any runs already made and the allowance shall be added to the score.

NOTES

1. If flags or posts are used to mark a boundary, the real or imaginary line joining such points shall be regarded as the boundary, which should be marked by a white line if possible.

2. In deciding on the allowances to be made for boundaries the umpires will be guided by the prevailing custom of the ground.

3. It is a 'Boundary' if the ball touches any boundary line or if a fieldsman with ball in hand grounds any part of his person on or over that line. A fieldsman, however, standing within the playing area may lean against or touch a boundary fence in fielding a ball. (*See also* Law 35, Note 5.)

4. An obstacle, or person, within the playing area is not regarded as a boundary unless so arranged by the umpires. The umpire is not a boundary, but sight screens within the playing area shall be so regarded.

5. The customary allowance for a boundary is 4 runs, but it is usual to allow 6 runs for all hits pitching over and clear of the boundary line or fence (even though the ball has been previously touched by a fieldsman). It is not usual to allow 6 runs when a ball hits a sight screen full pitch, if the latter is on or inside the boundary.

6. In the case of a boundary resulting from either an overthrow or the wilful act of a fieldsman, the run in progress counts provided that the batsmen have crossed at the instant of the throw or act.

7. The umpire signals 'Boundary' by waving an arm from side to side, or a boundary '6' by raising both arms above the head.

LOST BALL

21. If a ball in play cannot be found or recovered any Fieldsman may call 'Lost Ball', when 6 runs shall be added to the score; but if more than 6 have been run before 'Lost Ball' be called, as many runs as have been run shall be scored.

THE RESULT

22. A match is won by the side which shall have scored a total of runs in excess of that scored by the opposing side in its two completed innings; one-day matches, unless thus played out, shall be decided by the first innings. A match may also be determined by being given up as lost by one of the sides, or in the case governed by Law 17. A match not determined in any of these ways shall count as a 'Draw'.

NOTES

1. It is the responsibility of the captains to satisfy themselves on the correctness of the scores on the conclusion of play.

2. Neither side can be compelled to continue after a match is finished; a one-day match shall not be regarded as finished on the result of the first innings if the umpires consider there is a prospect of carrying the game to a further issue in the time remaining.

3. The result of a finished match is stated as a win by runs, except in the case of a win by the side batting last, when it is by the number of wickets still then to fall. In a one-day match which is not played out on the second innings, this rule applies to the position at the time when a result on the first innings was reached.

4. A 'Draw' is regarded as a 'Tie' when the scores

are equal at the conclusion of play but only if the match has been played out. If the scores of the completed first innings of a one-day match are equal, it is a 'Tie', but only if the match has not been played out to a further conclusion.

THE OVER

23. The ball shall be bowled from each wicket alternately in Overs of either 8 or 6 balls according to the agreed conditions of play. When the agreed number have been bowled and it has become clear to the Umpire at the Bowler's wicket that both sides have ceased to regard the ball as in play, the Umpire shall call 'Over' in a distinct manner before leaving the wicket. Neither a 'No Ball' nor a 'Wide Ball' shall be reckoned as one of the 'Over'.

NOTE

1. In the United Kingdom the 'over' shall be 6 balls, unless an agreement to the contrary has been made.

24. A Bowler shall finish an 'Over' in progress unless he be incapacitated or be suspended for unfair play. He shall be allowed to change ends as often as desired, provided only that he shall not bowl two 'Overs' consecutively in one innings. A Bowler may require the Batsman at the wicket from which he is bowling to stand on whichever side of it he may direct.

DEAD BALL

25. The ball shall be held to be 'Dead'—on being in the opinion of the Umpire finally settled in the hands of the Wicket-keeper or of the Bowler; or on reaching or pitching over the boundary; or,

whether played or not, on lodging in the dress of either a Batsman or Umpire; or on the call of 'Over' or 'Time' by the Umpire; or on a Batsman being out from any cause; or on any penalty being awarded under Laws 21 or 44. The Umpire shall call 'Dead Ball' should he decide to intervene under Law 46 in a case of unfair play or in the event of a serious injury to a player; or should he require to suspend play prior to the Striker receiving a delivery. The Ball shall cease to be 'Dead' on the Bowler starting his run or bowling action.

NOTES

1. Whether the ball is 'finally settled' is a question of fact for the umpire alone to decide.

2. An umpire is justified in suspending play prior to the striker receiving a delivery in any of the following circumstances:

(i) If satisfied that, for an *adequate* reason, the striker is not ready to receive the ball, and makes no attempt to play it.

(ii) If the bowler drops the ball accidentally before delivery, or if the ball does not leave his hand for any reason.

(iii) If one or both bails fall from the striker's wicket before he receives the delivery.

In such cases the ball is regarded as 'Dead' from the time it last came into play.

3. A ball does not become 'Dead' when it strikes an umpire (unless it lodges in his dress), when the wicket is broken or struck down (unless a batsman is out thereby), or when an unsuccessful appeal is made.

4. For the purpose of this and other Laws, the term 'dress' includes the equipment and clothing of players and umpires as normally worn.

NO BALL

26. For a delivery to be fair, the ball must be bowled not thrown. If either Umpire be not entirely satisfied of the absolute fairness of a delivery in this respect he shall call and signal 'No Ball' instantly upon delivery. The Umpire at the bowler's wicket shall call and signal 'No Ball' if, in the delivery stride, no part of the bowler's front foot is grounded behind the popping crease, or if he is not satisfied that the bowler's back foot has landed within and not touching the return crease or its forward extension.

NOTES

1. The striker is entitled to know whether the bowler intends to bowl over or round the wicket, overarm or underarm, right or left handed. An umpire may regard any failure to notify a change in the mode of delivery as 'unfair'; if so, he should call 'No ball.'

2. It is a 'No Ball' if the bowler before delivering a ball throws it at the striker's wicket even in an attempt to run him out. (*See* Law 46, Note 4 (vii).)

3. If a bowler break the near wicket with any part of his person during the delivery, such act in itself does not constitute 'No Ball.'

4. The umpire signals 'No Ball' by extending one arm horizontally.

5. An umpire should revoke the call 'No Ball' if the ball does not leave the bowler's hand for any reason.

27. The ball does not become 'Dead' on the call of 'No Ball'. The Striker may hit a 'No Ball' and whatever runs result shall be added to his score, but runs made otherwise from a 'No Ball' shall be scored 'No Balls', and if no runs be made one run shall be so scored. The Striker shall be out from a

'No Ball' if he break Law 37, and either Batsman may be run out, or given out if he break Laws 36 or 40.

NOTES

1. The penalty for a 'No Ball' is only scored if no runs result otherwise.

2. Law 46 Note 4 (vii) covers attempts to run before the ball is delivered, but should the non-striker unfairly leave his ground too soon, the fielding side may run out the batsman at the bowler's end by any recognized method. If the bowler throws at the near wicket, the umpire does not call 'No Ball', though any runs resulting are so scored. The throw does not count in the 'Over'.

WIDE BALL

28. If the Bowler shall bowl the ball so high over or so wide of the wicket that in the opinion of the Umpire it passes out of reach of the Striker, and would not have been within his reach when taking guard in the normal position, the Umpire shall call and signal 'Wide Ball' as soon as it shall have passed the Striker.

NOTES

1. If a ball which the umpire considers to have been delivered comes to rest in front of the striker 'Wide' should not be called, and no runs should be added to the score unless they result from the striker hitting the ball which he has a right to do without interference by the fielding side. Should the fielding side interfere, the umpire is justified in replacing the ball where it came to rest and ordering the fieldsman to resume the places they occupied in the field before the ball was delivered.

2. The umpire signals 'Wide' by extending both arms horizontally.

3. An umpire should revoke the call if the striker hits a ball which has been called 'Wide'.

29. The ball does not become 'Dead' on the call of 'Wide Ball'. All runs that are run from a 'Wide Ball' shall be scored 'Wide Balls', or if no runs be made one run shall be so scored. The Striker may be out from a 'Wide Ball' if he breaks Laws 38 or 42, and either Batsman may be run out, or given out if he break Laws 36 or 40.

BYE AND LEG BYE

30. If the ball, not having been called 'Wide' or 'No Ball', pass the Striker without touching his bat or person, and any runs be obtained, the Umpire shall call or signal 'Bye'; but if the ball touch any part of the Striker's dress or person except his hand holding the bat, and any run be obtained, the Umpire shall call or signal 'Leg Bye'; such runs to be scored 'Byes' and 'Leg Byes', respectively.

NOTES

1. The umpire shall regard the deliberate deflection of the ball by any part of the striker's person, except the hand holding the bat, as unfair, and as soon as he is satisfied that the fielding side have no chance of dismissing either batsman as an immediate result of such action, he shall, without delay, call 'dead ball'. In deciding whether such deflection is deliberate, the criterion shall be whether or not the batsman has attempted to play the ball with his bat.

2. The umpire signals 'Bye' by raising an open hand above the head, and 'Leg Bye' by touching a raised knee with the hand.

THE WICKET IS DOWN

31. The wicket shall be held to be 'Down' if either the ball or the Striker's bat or person completely removes either bail from the top of the stumps or, if both bails be off, strikes a stump out of the ground. Any player may use his hand or arm to put the wicket down or, even should the bails be previously off, may pull up a stump, provided always that the ball is held in the hand or hands so used.

NOTES

1. A wicket is not 'down' merely on account of the disturbance of a bail, but it is 'down' if a bail in falling from the wicket lodges between two of the stumps.

2. If one bail is off, it is sufficient for the purpose of this Law to dislodge the remaining one in any of the ways stated, or to strike any of the three stumps out of the ground.

3. If, owing to the strength of the wind, the captains have agreed to dispense with the use of bails (*see* Law 8, Note 2), the decision as to when the wicket is 'down' is one for the umpires to decide on the facts before them. In such circumstances the wicket be held to be 'down' even though a stump has not been struck out of the ground.

4. If the wicket is broken while the ball is in play, it is not the umpire's duty to remake the wicket until the ball has become 'dead.' A fieldsman, however, may remake the wicket in such circumstances.

5. For the purpose of this and other Laws the term 'person' includes a player's dress as defined in Law 25, Note 4.

OUT OF HIS GROUND

32. A Batsman shall be held to be 'Out of his ground' unless some part of his bat in hand or of his person be grounded behind the line of the Popping Crease.

BATSMAN RETIRING

33. A Batsman may retire at any time, but may not resume his innings without the consent of the opposing Captain, and then only on the fall of a wicket.

NOTE

1. When a batsman has retired owing to illness, injury or some other unavoidable cause, his innings is recorded as 'Retired, Not out', but otherwise as a completed innings to be recorded as 'Retired, Out'.

BOWLED

34. The Striker is out 'Bowled'—If the wicket be bowled down, even if the ball first touch his bat or person.

NOTES

1. The striker, after playing the ball, is out 'Bowled' if he then kicks or hits it on to his wicket before the completion of his stroke.

2. The striker is out 'Bowled' under this Law when the ball is deflected on to his wicket off his person, even though a decision against him might be justified under Law 39 L.B.W.

CAUGHT

35. The Striker is out 'Caught'—If the ball, from a stroke of the bat or of the hand holding the bat,

but not the wrist, be held by a Fieldsman before it touch the ground, although it be hugged to the body of the catcher, or be accidentally lodged in his dress. The Fieldsman must have both his feet entirely within the playing area at the instant the catch is completed.

NOTES

1. Provided the ball does not touch the ground, the hand holding it may do so in effecting a catch.

2. The umpire is justified in disregarding the fact that the ball has touched the ground, or has been carried over the boundary provided that a catch has in fact been completed prior to such occurrence.

3. The fact that a ball has touched the striker's person before or after touching his bat does not invalidate a catch.

4. The striker may be 'Caught' even if the fieldsman has not touched the ball with his hands, including the case of a ball lodging in the wicket-keeper's pads.

5. A fieldsman standing within the playing area may lean against a boundary to catch a ball, and this may be done even if the ball has passed over the boundary.

6. If the striker lawfully plays the ball a second time he may be out under this Law, but only if the ball has not touched the ground since being first struck.

7. The striker may be caught off any obstruction within the playing area provided it has not previously been decided on as a boundary.

HANDLED THE BALL

36. Either Batsman is out 'Handled the Ball'—If he touch it while in play with his hands, unless it be done at the request of the opposite side.

NOTES

1. A hand holding the bat is regarded as part of it for the purposes of Laws 36, 37, and 39.

2. The correct entry in the score book when a batsman is given out under this Law is 'Handled the Ball', and the bowler does not get credit for the wicket.

HIT THE BALL TWICE

37. The Striker is out 'Hit the ball twice'—If the ball be struck or be stopped by any part of his person, and he wilfully strike it again, except for the sole purpose of guarding his wicket, which he may do with his bat or any part of his person, other than his hands. No runs except those which result from an overthrow shall be scored from a ball lawfully struck twice.

NOTES

1. It is for the umpire to decide whether the ball has been so struck a second time legitimately or not. The umpire may regard the fact that a run is attempted as evidence of the batsmen's intention to take advantage of the second stroke, but it is not conclusive.

2. A batsman may not attempt to hit the ball twice if in so doing he baulks the wicket-keeper or any fieldsman attempting to make a catch.

3. This Law is infringed if the striker, after playing the ball and without any request from the opposite side, uses his bat to return the ball to a fieldsman.

4. The correct entry in the score book when the striker is given out under this Law is 'Hit the ball twice', and the bowler does not get credit for the wicket.

HIT WICKET

38. The striker is out 'Hit wicket'—If in playing at the ball he hit down his wicket with his bat or any part of his person.

NOTES

1. The striker is 'Out' under this Law if:
 (i) In making a second stroke to keep the ball out of his wicket he hits it down.
 (ii) While playing at the ball, but not otherwise, his wicket is broken by his cap or hat falling, or by part of his bat.

2. A batsman is not out for breaking the wicket with his bat or person while in the act of running.

L.B.W.

39. The Striker is out 'Leg before wicket'—If with any part of his person except his hand, which is in a straight line between wicket and wicket, even though the point of impact be above the level of the bails, he intercept a ball which has not first touched his bat or hand, and which, in the opinion of the Umpire, shall have, or would have, pitched on a straight line from the Bowler's wicket to the Striker's wicket, or shall have pitched on the off-side of the Striker's wicket, provided always that the ball would have hit the wicket.

NOTES

1. The word 'hand' used in this Law should be interpreted as the hand holding the bat.

2. A batsman is only 'Out' under this Law if *all* the four following questions are answered in the affirmative.
 (i) Would the ball have hit the wicket?

(ii) Did the ball pitch on a straight line between wicket and wicket (and this case includes a ball intercepted full pitch by the striker), or did it pitch on the offside of the striker's wicket?

(iii) Was it part of the striker's person other than the hand which first intercepted the ball?

(iv) Was that part of the striker's person in a straight line between wicket and wicket at the moment of impact irrespective of the height of the point of impact?

OBSTRUCTING THE FIELD

40. Either Batsman is out 'Obstructing the field' —If he wilfully obstruct the opposite side; should such wilful obstruction by either Batsman prevent a ball from being caught it is the Striker who is out.

NOTES

1. The umpire must decide whether the obstruction was 'wilful' or not. The involuntary interception by a batsman while running of a throw in is not in itself an offence.

2. The correct entry in the score book when a batsman is given out under this Law is 'Obstructing the field', and the bowler does not get credit for the wicket.

RUN OUT

41. Either Batsman is out 'Run out'—If in running or at any time, while the ball is in play, he be out of his ground, and his wicket be put down by the opposite side. If the batsmen have crossed each other, he that runs for the wicket which is put down is out; if they have not crossed, he that has

left the wicket which is put down is out. But unless
he attempt to run, the Striker shall not be given
'Run out' in the circumstances stated in Law 42,
even should 'No Ball' have been called.

NOTE

1. If the ball is played on to the opposite wicket,
neither batsman is liable to be 'Run out' unless the ball
has been touched by a fieldsman before the wicket is put
down.

STUMPED

42. A Striker is out 'Stumped'—If in receiving a
ball, not being a 'No Ball', delivered by the Bowler,
he be out of his ground otherwise than in attempting a run, and the wicket be put down by the
Wicket-keeper without the intervention of another
fieldsman. Only when the ball has touched the bat
or person of the Striker may the Wicket-keeper
take it in front of the wicket for this purpose.

NOTE

1. The striker may be 'Stumped' if the wicket is
broken by a ball rebounding from the wicket-keeper's
person.

THE WICKET-KEEPER

43. The Wicket-keeper shall remain wholly
behind the wicket until a ball delivered by the
Bowler touches the bat or person of the Striker, or
passes the wicket, or until the Striker attempts a
run. Should the Wicket-keeper contravene this
Law, the Striker shall not be out except under
Laws 36, 37, 40 and 41 and then only subject to
Law 46.

NOTES

1. This Law is provided to secure to the striker his right to play the ball and to guard his wicket without interference from the wicket-keeper. The striker may not be penalized if in the legitimate defence of his wicket he interferes with the wicket-keeper, except as provided for in Law 37, Note 2.

2. If, in the opinion of the umpire, the encroachment by the wicket-keeper has not gained any advantage for the fielding side, nor in any way has interfered with the right of the striker to play the ball with complete freedom, nor has had any effect whatsoever on the dismissal of the striker, he shall disregard the infringement.

THE FIELDSMAN

44. The Fieldsman may stop the ball with any part of his person, but if he wilfully stop it otherwise five runs shall be added to the run or runs already made; if no run has been made five shall be scored. The penalty shall be added to the score of the Striker if the ball has been struck, but otherwise to the score of Byes, Leg Byes, No Balls or Wides as the case may be.

NOTES

1. A fieldsman must not use his cap, etc., for the purpose of fielding a ball.

2. The five runs are a penalty and the batsmen do not change ends.

3. The number of on-side fielders behind the popping crease at the instant of the bowler's delivery shall not exceed two. In the event of infringement by the fielding side, the square-leg Umpire shall call 'No Ball'.

Note: The Umpire may elect to stand on the off side,

provided he informs the Captain of the fielding side and the Striker of his intention to do so.

(E) DUTIES OF THE UMPIRES

45. Before the toss for innings, the Umpires shall acquaint themselves with any 'Special Regulations', and shall agree with both Captains on any other conditions affecting the conduct of the match; shall satisfy themselves that the wickets are properly pitched; and shall agree between themselves on the watch or clock to be followed during play.

NOTES

1. Apart from 'Special Regulations' other conditions of play within the framework of the Laws are frequently necessary, *e.g.* Hours of play, Intervals, etc.

2. The captains are entitled to know which clock or watch will be followed during play.

46. Before and during a match the Umpires shall ensure that the conduct of the game and the implements used are strictly in accordance with the Laws; they are the sole judges of fair and unfair play, and the final judges of the fitness of the ground, the weather and the light for play in the event of the decision being left to them; all disputes shall be determined by them, and if they disagree the actual state of things shall continue. The Umpires shall change ends after each side has had one innings.

NOTES

1. An umpire should stand where he can best see any act upon which his decision may be required. Subject to

this over-riding consideration the umpire at the bowler's end should stand where he does not interfere with either the bowler's run up or the striker's view. If the other umpire wishes to stand on the off instead of the leg side of the pitch he should obtain the permission of the captain of the fielding side and inform the batsman.

2. The umpires must not allow the attitude of the players or spectators to influence their decisions under the Laws.

3. A code of signals for umpires is laid down in Notes to the relevant Laws; but an umpire must call as well as signal, if necessary, to inform the players and scorers.

4. FAIR AND UNFAIR PLAY

(i) The umpires are entitled to intervene without appeal in the case of unfair play, but should not otherwise interfere with the progress of the game, except as required to do so by the Laws.

(ii) In the event of a player failing to comply with the instructions of an umpire or criticising his decisions, the umpires should in the first place request the captains to take action, and if this proves ineffective, report the incident forthwith to the executives of the teams taking part in the match.

(iii) It is illegal for a player to lift the seam of the ball in order to obtain a better hold. In such a case the umpire will if necessary change the ball for one which has had similar wear, and will warn the captain that the practice is unfair. The use of resin, wax, etc., by bowlers is also unfair, but a bowler may dry the ball when wet on a towel or with sawdust.

(iv) An umpire is justified in intervening under this Law should any player of the fielding side incommode the striker by any noise or motion while he is receiving a ball.

(v) It is the duty of umpires to intervene and prevent players from causing damage to the pitch which may assist the bowlers.

(vi) The persistent bowling of fast short-pitched balls at the batsman is unfair if, in the opinion of the umpire at the bowler's end, it constitutes a systematic attempt at intimidation. In such event he must adopt the following procedure:

(a) When he decides that such bowling is becoming persistent he forthwith 'cautions' the bowler.

(b) If this 'caution' is ineffective, he informs the captain of the fielding side and the other umpire of what has occurred.

(c) Should the above prove ineffective, the umpire at the bowler's end must:

(i) At the first repetition call 'Dead Ball,' when the over is regarded as completed.

(ii) Direct the captain of the fielding side to take the bowler off forthwith. The captain shall take the bowler off as directed.

(iii) Report the occurrence to the captain of the batting side as soon as an interval of play takes place.

A bowler who has been 'taken off' as above may not bowl again during the same innings.

(vii) Any attempt by the batsmen to *steal a run* during the bowler's run up is unfair. Unless the bowler throws the ball at either wicket (*see* Laws 26, Note 2, and 27, Note 2), the umpire should call 'Dead Ball' as soon as the batsmen cross in any such attempt to run, after which they return to their original wickets.

(viii) No player shall leave the field for the purpose of having a rub down or shower while play is actually in progress.

5. GROUND, WEATHER AND LIGHT

(i) Unless agreement to the contrary is made before the start of a match, the captains (during actual play the batsmen at the wickets may deputize for their captain) may elect to decide in regard to the fitness of the ground, weather or light for play; otherwise or in the event of disagreement, the umpires are required to decide.

(ii) Play should only be suspended when the conditions are so bad that it is unreasonable or dangerous for it to continue. The ground is unfit for play when water stands on the surface or when it is so wet or slippery as to deprive the batsmen or bowlers of a reasonable foothold, or the fieldsmen of power of free movement. Play should *not* be suspended merely because the grass is wet and the ball slippery.

(iii) After any suspension of play, the captains, or, if the decision has been left to them, the umpires, unaccompanied by any of the players, will without further instructions carry out an inspection immediately the conditions improve, and will continue to inspect at intervals. Immediately the responsible parties decide that play is possible, they must call upon the players to resume the game.

APPEALS

47. The Umpires shall not order a Batsman out unless appealed to by the other side which shall be done prior to the delivery of the next ball, and before 'Time' is called under Law 18. The Umpire at the Bowler's wicket shall answer appeals before the other Umpire in all cases except those arising

out of Laws 38 or 42 and out of Law 41 for run out at the Striker's wicket. In any case in which an Umpire is unable to give a decision, he shall appeal to the other Umpire whose decision shall be final.

NOTES

1. An appeal, 'How's that?' covers all ways of being out (within the jurisdiction of the umpire appealed to), unless a specific way of getting out is stated by the person asking. When either umpire has given a batsman 'Not out' the other umpire may answer any appeal within his jurisdiction, provided it is made in time.

2. The umpire signals 'Out' by raising the index finger above the head. If the batsman is not out, the umpire calls 'Not out'.

3. An umpire may alter his decision provided that such alteration is made promptly.

4. Nothing in this Law prevents an umpire before giving a decision from consulting the other umpire on a point of fact which the latter may have been in a better position to observe. An umpire should not appeal to the other umpire in cases on which he could give a decision, merely because he is unwilling to give that decision. If after consultation he is still in any doubt, the principle laid down in Law 46 applies and the decision will be in favour of the batsman.

5. The umpires should intervene if satisfied that a batsman, not having been given out, has left his wicket under a misapprehension.

6. Under Law 25 the ball is 'Dead' on 'Over' being called; this does not invalidate an appeal made prior to the first ball of the following 'Over', provided the bails have not been removed by both umpires after 'Time' has been called.

NOTES FOR SCORERS AND UMPIRES

1. (*a*) Law 4 explains the status of the scorers in relation to the umpires.

(*b*) During the progress of the game, if two scorers have been appointed, they should frequently check the total to ensure that the score sheets agree.

(*c*) The following method of entering 'No Balls' and 'Wides' (Laws 27 and 29) in the score sheet is recommended:

 (i) If no run is scored from the bat off a 'No Ball', the latter should be entered as an 'Extra', and a dot placed in the bowling analysis with a circle round it to show that the ball does not count in the over.

 (ii) If runs are scored from the bat off a 'No Ball', they should be credited to the striker, and entered in the bowling analysis with a circle round the figure. Such runs count against the bowler in his analysis even though the ball does not count in the over.

 (iii) All runs scored from 'Wide Balls' are entered as 'Extras', and inserted in the bowler's analysis with a cross to indicate that the ball does not count in the over.

2. The following code of signalling between the umpires and the scorers has been approved:

Boundaries—by waving the hand from side to side.

A boundary six—by raising both arms above the head.

Byes—by raising the open hand above the head.

Leg Byes—by touching a raised knee with the hand.

Wides—by extending both arms horizontally.

No Balls—by extending one arm horizontally.

The decision 'Out'—by raising the index finger above the head.

'One Short'—by bending the arm upwards and by touching the top of the nearest shoulder with the tips of the fingers of one hand.

3. If the above instructions are properly carried out, cases of disagreement as regards the scores and the results of matches should not occur.

It is, however, important that the captains should satisfy themselves of the correctness of the scores on the conclusion of play, as errors cannot subsequently be corrected.

It should be noted that, in general, by accepting the result notified by the scorers, the captain of the losing side has thereby acquiesced in the 'playing out or giving up' of the match as stated in Law 22.

REGULATIONS FOR DRYING THE PITCH AND GROUND IN FIRST-CLASS MATCHES

N.B.: *These regulations are primarily designed for First-class Cricket, and their application in whole or in part in other grades of Cricket is at the discretion of the ground, etc., authorities.*

1. Except as provided below, the existing regulations in regard to the rolling of the pitch and the fitness of the ground for play shall apply. (*See* Laws 10, 12 and 46.)

2. (i) To enable play to proceed with the least possible delay after rain, the groundsman shall adopt every practical means to protect or rid the surface of the ground, *other than the pitch*, of water or dampness at any time except while play is in progress.

(ii) Prior to tossing for choice of innings the artificial drying of the pitch and outfield shall be at the discretion of the Groundsman. Thereafter and throughout the match the drying of the outfield may be undertaken at any time by the Groundsman, but the drying of the pitch shall be carried out only on the instructions and under the supervision of the Umpires. The Umpires shall be empowered to have the pitch dried without a reference to the Captains at any time they are of the opinion that it is unfit for play.

(iii) In wet weather, the Umpires shall see that the footholes made by the bowlers and batsmen are cleaned, dried and filled up with sawdust at any time during the match, although the game is not actually in progress.

The Groundsman, without instructions from the Umpires, may also clean out in this way foot-holes, provided they are not on any part of the pitch, more than 3 ft 6 in in front of the Popping creases.

The drying of the footholds on the pitch itself may be undertaken, as directed by the Umpires, at any time. The Umpires may also direct the Groundsman to protect against further rain marks made by the bowlers, even though they be more than 3 ft 6 in in front of the popping creases, provided they are not between wicket and wicket, with loose sawdust, which, however, shall be removed prior to the resumption of play.

(iv) The Umpires shall ascertain from the Groundsman before the commencement of a match what equipment is available for drying the pitch artificially.

Any roller may be used, if the Umpires think desirable, but only (except as laid down in paragraph (2) (v)) for the purpose of drying the pitch and making it fit for play, and not otherwise. This would allow Umpires to roll the pitch after drying it, say with a light roller, for a minute or two, should they consider it desirable.

(v) When the artificial drying of the pitch under the supervision of the Umpires, coincides with any interval during the match, after the toss for choice of innings, the Umpires and not the Captain of the batting side shall select the roller to be used.

(vi) The fact that the Umpires may have dried the pitch artificially does not take the decision as regards the fitness of the pitch and ground for play out of the hands of the Captains even though the Umpires may have selected the roller to be used for the drying process. Law 46, Note 5 (i) is applicable in such cases.

INDEX TO THE LAWS OF CRICKET